Writing to Learn

AN INTRODUCTION TO WRITING PHILOSOPHICAL ESSAYS

Anne Michaels Edwards

Boston   Burr Ridge, IL   Dubuque, IA   Madison, WI
New York   San Francisco   St. Louis
Bangkok   Bogotá   Caracas   Lisbon   London   Madrid   Mexico City
Milan   New Delhi   Seoul   Singapore   Sydney   Taipei   Toronto

McGraw-Hill Higher Education

*A Division of The **McGraw-Hill** Companies*

WRITING TO LEARN
AN INTRODUCTION TO WRITING PHILOSOPHICAL ESSAYS

This book is printed on acid-free paper.

1 2 3 4 5 6 7 8 9 0 FGR/FGR 9 0 9 8 7 6 5 4 3 2 1 0 9

ISBN 0-07-365504-X

Vice president/Editor-in-chief: *Thalia Dorwick*
Editorial director: *Jane Vaicunas/Phillip A. Butcher*
Sponsoring editor: *Monica Eckman/Sarah Touborg Moyers*
Senior marketing manager: *Daniel M. Loch*
Senior project manager: *Susan Trentacosti*
Manager, new book production: *Melonie Salvati*
Freelance design coordinator: *Pam Verros*
Cover photograph: © *Photodisc*
Compositor: *Electronic Publishing Services, Inc., TN*
Typeface: *10/12 Aster*
Printer: *Quebecor Printing Book Group/Fairfield*

Library of Congress Cataloging-in-Publication Data

Edwards, Anne Michaels.
  Writing to learn : an introduction to writing philosophical essays
/ by Anne Michaels Edwards.
    p.   cm.
  ISBN 0-07-365504-X (alk. paper)
  1. Philosophy—Authorship.   I. Title.
B52.7.E38   2000
808'.0661—dc21   99-37746

http://www.mhhe.com

CONTENTS

ACKNOWLEDGMENTS

Thanks are due to many of my colleagues and students for their help in the preparation of this manuscript. Thanks also to my editor, Sarah Moyers, for encouraging me to write this book. And, as always, for Mark, my *sine qua non*.

Anne Michaels Edwards

1

INTRODUCTION

The purpose of this book is, quite simply, to teach you how to write philosophical essays. It is based largely on the premise that one of the best ways for a student to understand a topic is to be required to write about it. Most of the work in a philosophy class involves reading assigned material, thinking about it, and then writing about it—whether on an exam or in an essay written outside of class. This book is intended to make all three of those activities easier. However, this book is not for philosophers only. While it should prove helpful in any philosophy class, regardless of teacher, subject, or textbook, you will be able to apply many of the guidelines to almost any paper or essay exam you are assigned in almost any college course.

There is so much about writing that a student needs to know, and so little time for an instructor to teach it. Most teachers want to focus on their subject (in this case, philosophy) and not on the task of writing. Although this book is not intended as a substitute for the instructor, it can be a valuable supplement for anyone enrolled in a philosophy course. If you have taken one or more philosophy classes already, then you may already know some of what is in this book. While the emphasis is on the kind of essays typically assigned in introductory philosophy classes, most of these same kinds of essays are assigned in upper-level courses as well.

If this is your first philosophy class, many of the names and theories will be unfamiliar to you. I have tried to include as many of them as possible in the glossary. However, don't be intimidated by things you don't know. As you are reading this book, should you come across a name, concept, or word you aren't familiar with, look it up in the glossary. In most instances, you will not need to know the people or the theories mentioned in order to understand the point being made.

This is meant to be a practical book. While your instructor may make use of this book in class, it is intended to be used with no interpretation or explanation necessary. Almost every philosophy class involves writing assignments of varying difficulty. *Writing to Learn* is meant to help you fulfill these assignments better, and, with luck, to earn a good grade in the process. The kinds of essays covered in Chapters 3, 4, and 5 are usually found only on examinations. Papers assigned by your instructor will probably be like those discussed in Chapters 6, 7, and 8. Even if your instructor doesn't assign out-of-class papers, chances are good that on exams, quizzes, or in-class essays, you will be required to write one or more of these kinds of essays.

Chapters 3 through 7 will guide you through several different types of essays, beginning with the simplest summaries, which demonstrate knowledge and understanding, and progressing through essays that require the application of theories to new situations, the analysis of the arguments used, the evaluation of those arguments, and finally, the synthesis of several theories or arguments.[1] One chapter is devoted to each of these levels of knowledge, illustrating the kind of reasoning necessary and helping you to write an essay at that level. Clearly, you must accomplish the easier levels of reasoning before you can progress to the ones that are more difficult.

What this means is that, while each chapter can be used independently ("My instructor assigned an evaluative essay, I'd better read Chapter 6"), each chapter builds on the previous chapters. For example, you can't write an evaluative essay until you can first write a summary as well as an analysis of what you want to evaluate. Therefore, your best bet is to read the book straight through. However, for those of you who won't do that because of time constraints or general disinclination, some hints follow in the section below.

Writing an essay is a good way to develop your ideas on a topic. By attempting to express an idea in your own words, you gain a deeper and more complete understanding than if you merely read what someone else has written. Thus, philosophy is something you *do*—it is not a collection of facts to be learned or equations to be applied. When you "do philosophy," as we like to say, you are actively reading, thinking, and writing. And this is the only way to "do" philosophy. No one can "teach" it to you—you have to "learn" it yourself. You must, then, take these words about teaching to heart:

> It is obvious that teaching is a very special art, sharing with only two other arts—agriculture and medicine—an exceptionally important characteristic. A doctor may do many things for his patient, but in the final analysis it is the patient himself who must get well—grow in health. The farmer does many things for his plants or animals, but in the final analysis it is they that must grow in size and excellence. Similarly, although the teacher may help his students in many ways, it is the student himself who must do the learning. Knowledge must grow in his mind if learning is to take place.[2]

---

[1] I am obviously indebted to Benjamin Bloom, et al., *Taxonomy of Educational Objectives: The Classifications of Educational Goals. Handbook I: Cognitive Domain* (New York: Longman Publishing, 1980).

[2] Mortimer J. Adler and Charles Van Doren, *How to Read a Book* (New York: Touchstone Books, 1972), pp. 12–13.

HOW TO USE THIS BOOK

For those students unable to read this text in its entirety, the following overview should help to identify when and how each of the chapters will be most useful.

Chapter 2: Reading Philosophy

This book begins in Chapter 2 with some helpful hints on how to read philosophy. You should certainly read this chapter before you read anything else. Because the content of a course is generally found in the readings, and because most often you are asked to write about something that you have read, it is very important that you read carefully and well. If you can't understand what you are reading, you can't write about it. Reading philosophy is probably unlike reading anything else you encounter. It requires slow reading, extensive rereading, and can be made easier by using certain techniques. This chapter won't make reading philosophy easy, but it should make it easier.

Chapter 3: Writing for Understanding

If your instructor is giving an essay exam, *be sure* you read Chapter 3 on writing for understanding (and also see Appendix A on taking essay exams). Whatever else an instructor asks you to do, he is sure to ask you to *summarize* some essay or theory. (Of course, you will probably be asked to do more than that, but *at least* you must be able to do this much.) For example, a typical question on an Introduction to Philosophy exam might read:

> In the *First Meditation,* what three reasons does Descartes give for doubting? Explain *why* he thinks they are reasons for doubting everything you know.

This question requires you to summarize not only Descartes's conclusions, but also his arguments for those conclusions. Any question that asks for a definition also requires a summary. For example:

> What is William Paley's argument for the existence of God?
>
> What are Aristotle's four causes?
>
> What is the *tabula rasa* theory of the intellect?

While these may be only the *first* part of the question (for example, the question about Paley may go on to ask if you agree with him), without being able to put the arguments and theories into your own words, you will not be able to answer the rest of the question.

Chapter 4: Writing for Application

If your instructor asks you to *apply* some theory to a new situation, head straight for Chapter 4. An application question typically looks something like this:

What is Mill's principle of utility? Using Kant's example of whether you should tell the truth to a murderer about the location of the one he wishes to murder, explain what you think Mill would say you should do, and why.

Notice that first it asks you to summarize Mill's principle of utility (which is why you need to understand Chapter 3 first). Then it asks you to apply his theory to a particular example. Other examples, which would also require you to first summarize a theory (although they may not explicitly say so), are these:

What do you think Locke would say about the identity of a person with amnesia? That is, is she the same person she was before she got amnesia?

What are the four Aristotelian causes of a piece of chocolate cake?

Explain Kant's distinction between perfect and imperfect duties. Provide examples of each.

First you must say, "Here is what the theory or definition is," and then, "And here is how that applies to a person with amnesia, a piece of chocolate cake, or whatever." As you can see, you are unlikely to have any question that is *purely* summary or application.

Chapter 5: Writing for Analysis

If your instructor asks you to *analyze* an argument, Chapter 5 will show you how to examine ideas and theories and break them into their component parts. The chapter talks about argument form and common argumentative mistakes and discusses how to separate facts from opinions, necessary from probable conclusions, and assumptions from logical conclusions. Analysis involves not only explaining an author's conclusion, but also his reasons for believing his conclusion and how he argues for his conclusion. An analysis question might ask:

How does Descartes reach his conclusion at the end of the *Second Meditation* that the one thing he can be sure of is that he exists?

Not only must you be able to say what Descartes's conclusion is and what his reasons for it are (summary), but you must be prepared to analyze his argument. Other examples include:

What is Mill's argument regarding the connection between justice and utility?

Discuss Descartes's meditation on the ball of wax. What is it intended to show?

How does Plato try to argue that there are three distinct parts of the soul?

Chapter 6: Writing for Evaluation

Turn to Chapter 6 when you must write the most common essay assigned in philosophy classes, the *evaluative essay*. An evaluative essay requires that you first summarize and analyze an argument, and then evaluate it. Is the author right? Why or why not? Do her reasons support her conclusion? In an evaluative essay, you are essentially arguing for a position. Clearly, if you have not learned to write the earlier types of essays, this kind of essay can be impossibly hard and largely incomprehensible. The following are typical evaluative questions:

Does Paley's design argument prove the existence of the Judeo-Christian God? Why or why not?

Explicate and discuss John Locke's concept of *tabula rasa*. What are the strengths of this view? What are its weaknesses?

Explain Hume's reasoning for remaining skeptical of reports of miracles. Is this reasoning sound?

Present and evaluate Descartes's proof of his own existence.

Chapter 7: Writing for Synthesis

If none of the earlier chapters match what your instructor has asked you to do, turn to Chapter 7—*synthesis essays*. *Synthesis* involves bringing together parts and elements of several theories to create a new whole that requires original thinking. A typical synthesis question might read like this:

Do universals like Truth and Beauty really exist? Provide an argument to support your answer.

Or:

Is it morally permissible to use nonhuman animals to test products intended for human use? Why or why not?

Or (everyone's favorite):

What is the meaning of life?

These questions ask you to create your *own* argument for a particular conclusion. Notice that synthesis essays, like evaluative essays, are argumentative. That is, you are arguing that your theory is the correct one. This is, in some ways, the hardest kind of essay to write. Although some students instinctively want to take the best of several theories to make one they feel is better, many find it hard to think creatively in this way. However, remember, you can't expect to write a good synthesis essay if you cannot write a good summary, application, analysis, and evaluation.

Chapter 8: Using Research in a Philosophy Paper

If you are expected to do research for your paper, read Chapter 8. You will probably also need to read Chapter 6 and possibly Chapter 7, since most research papers may also be evaluative or synthesis essays. And, of course, you should probably understand Chapter 5, in order to analyze what you read. In general, I tell students that if they have read anything other than their textbook in preparing their essays, then they need to follow the guidelines for a research essay. Chapter 8 covers the use of sources and quotations and the proper form for footnotes and bibliographies.

Chapter 9: Putting Pencil to Paper (or Fingers to Keyboard)

Chapter 9 contains suggestions on how to get started as well as a discussion of the mechanics of the essay. There is advice about following directions, writing the kind of essay assigned, using the right paper, margins, fonts, and so on. Chapter 9 also emphasizes the need for rewriting, rewriting, and rewriting some more! While most of the information about first drafts is in the respective chapters, this chapter offers guidance on how to avoid common mistakes (like sexist language and some common fallacies), as well as editing and proofreading. At the very least, you should read Chapter 9 before writing any philosophical essay.

Appendixes

The text concludes with three appendixes. Appendix A has some helpful hints on how to take essay exams. Appendix B contains an annotated bibliography of philosophical resources especially helpful to introductory students (like *The Encyclopedia of Philosophy*, *The Philosopher's Index*, and various reference works that are easily accessible). It is not a very long list; rather, it includes just a few of the very best, most common and easily available resources you might use in the course of writing a philosophical essay. Appendix C is an extensive glossary of words, theories, names, movements, and so on that you might come into contact with in your philosophy course. In addition to key terms (which appear in boldface type in the chapters), it also includes brief definitions or designations of all the people and theories mentioned in the book.

Now you should have all the information you need—either to begin at the beginning and work straight through to the end, or else to go straight to the relevant chapter. Good luck!

2

READING PHILOSOPHY

Before you can write intelligibly about a subject, you must first *understand* the subject. Since most of the writing you are asked to do in philosophy classes will be about something you have read, it is essential that you learn to read philosophy well. Reading philosophy is different from anything you have ever read before. Unlike some of your other college textbooks, you cannot skim a philosophical essay for the main facts or details. You must read philosophy much more slowly than you would, say, a magazine or a novel. Philosophical essays are what philosophers like to call *dense* reading. That is, there are many ideas in a compact space. While you could probably get the sense of a novel by reading only every second or third paragraph, this kind of tactic would never work for philosophy. Sentence structure is often complex, and the topic may be one that you have never thought deeply about or one that you do not find particularly interesting. In addition, the fact that a philosophical essay is presenting an argument or explaining someone else's argument means that you must pay close attention to every part of the essay.

Also, some philosophical essays were written hundreds or even thousands of years ago. They rely on words, ideas, and assumptions that may have been clear at the time they were written, but are no longer clear to the modern reader. Some philosophical essays were written in other languages and have been translated. Sometimes the translations are bad ones; sometimes the translations are so accurate that they reflect the complexity of the original language a little too well for American readers (this is particularly true of some translations from German); and sometimes the original essay, whether in a foreign language or not, was not well written. It is sad, but true, that many philosophical essays are poorly written, contain confused or faulty arguments, and/or rest on assumptions and ideas that are either questionable or downright wrong.

Don't be surprised if you don't understand an essay the first time you read it. Don't even be surprised if you don't understand all of it the second time around. Reading philosophical essays requires a great deal of patience, concentration, and perseverance. With philosophy, you must read, reread, and then reread some more. Like any other skill, your ability to read philosophy will improve with practice.

TECHNIQUES FOR READING PHILOSOPHY

While philosophy is difficult reading, it is not impossible. This section presents some techniques that will make the task ahead of you easier.

Give Yourself Enough Time

Read the entire section or essay in one sitting. If you try to read your philosophy homework in 10- or 15-minute segments, you will not succeed. Because a philosophical essay almost always proposes a line of reasoning, if you stop in the middle you run the risk of forgetting what came before. While this is not fatal if you are reading a novel or a magazine article, it is for a philosophical essay. Not only do you have to *read* the whole essay, but you have to *understand* it too. A large part of that understanding involves following the process of the author's reasoning. So give yourself plenty of time to read completely through the assignment.

Use All Available Study Aids

If your reading is from a textbook, make good use of all the study aids the author or editor offers. Read the preface or introduction to the book. Read chapter and essay introductions or summaries. Examine the study questions to get an idea of what the important points probably are. Take advantage of any section headings, margin notes, and boxed passages if your textbook offers them. Make liberal use of the glossary, if there is one, and the index. If the book has a detailed table of contents, study it. Skim the reading first to spot any headings or emphasized passages. All of these are instructional features that can help you read the book more easily. Most of the philosophical readings that you will be assigned will contain one or more of these features. Take advantage of them!

Grant All Ideas a Fair Hearing

One good rule to follow when you are reading philosophy is what is called the **principle of charity.** If your instructor has asked you to read an essay, he most likely thinks that there is something valuable to be learned from the essay. Be charitable. Give the authors the benefit of the doubt. Even if you think they are wrong, try to be very clear about *what* you think they are saying and *why* you think they are mistaken. Grant all ideas a fair hearing, even if (especially if) you don't agree with them. People have the most trouble understanding and remembering ideas they disagree with, so this is something to work on.

Read and Reread

You can rarely read a philosophical essay just once and completely understand it. Philosophical writing demands careful, slow, and repeated reading. You will probably have to read the entire essay at least twice, and some individual passages you may need to read several more times. Reread as often as you need to, to understand what the author is saying. However, don't spend so much time rereading a passage that you get discouraged. If you really can't understand a particular section or passage, flag it and come back to it later. After you have read further, you may find that your understanding has improved, and you can now reread passages you didn't understand with more comprehension.

Change Your Surroundings

If you are experiencing a great deal of frustration or difficulty with your philosophy reading, consider finding a new place to read. If you are tired, distracted, uncomfortable, hungry, thirsty, or whatever, you may have difficulties with your reading. The better you can make the atmosphere, the better your comprehension is likely to be.

Read Actively

Philosophy must be read actively—that is, you must be constantly asking yourself: What is the main point? Why did the author just say that? What are the author's reasons for believing this? Do I agree or disagree with this point? Keep a pencil, a highlighter, a pad of sticky notes, or a note pad handy. Mark passages that seem important, or passages that you don't understand. However, don't highlight every sentence! In fact, don't underline or highlight at all on your first reading, except to mark passages you don't understand. Only on the second reading should you begin to mark up the text (and then only if you own the book); otherwise take notes. Also, annotate as you read. Comments may be as simple as "huh?" or "yes!" They may be your thoughts on why the author is wrong, or they may indicate how what the author says connects with something else that you've read. Use your notes to ask questions, to mark passages you don't understand, or to indicate where you agree or disagree and what you think are the significant parts of the essay.

Keep a Dictionary Handy

Merriam-Webster's Collegiate Dictionary[1] is a good comprehensive dictionary that can often be found on sale for a reasonable price. A paperback pocket dictionary probably will not be adequate. Philosophers, like other scholars, tend to use large and sometimes obscure words. Occasionally you can get the meaning from the context of the essay, but often you can't. Philosophers also use many technical terms that you will not find in even a very good dictionary. Some of the words are unique to philosophy; others (like "substance" or "material") look common but have different or more specific meanings for philosophers. So using a good dictionary is critical. Use any philosophy dictionaries available, or consult an encyclopedia of philosophy (see Appendix B). However, when you are just trying to read for understanding, a good dictionary and the glossary should be sufficient.

Stop and Summarize What You Have Read

After you finish a section or a page, pause and see if you can restate what the author is saying in your own words. If you cannot do so, then you do not understand what you have read. Summarizing is described at length in Chapter 3, but here is a short overview. As you read, regularly stop, close your eyes, and mentally summarize the main points of what you have read. If you are ambitious, actually writing your summary down is even better, since it helps you remember what you've read. This does not mean merely paraphrasing some sentences or the section headings. It means figuring out what the *most important* parts of the essay or argument are and restating them so that you know that you understand them—and are not merely parroting what you have read.

Look for the Essay's Main Points

On your first reading of an essay, you should be looking for the author's **conclusions.** Ask yourself, What is the author trying to prove? Just grasping the main points is a large part of the battle. Don't try to understand every sentence the first time through. If there are passages or details that you find particularly difficult even after reading them several times, skip over them and go on. Perhaps by the next time through you'll understand them better. If you spend too much time trying to figure out the fine points, you may completely miss the main points.

Identify the Essay's Premises

Once you understand the point or points the author is trying to prove, you need to figure out what her *reasons* are. On your second reading, ask yourself, *Why* does she think her conclusion is true? As a rule, a philosophical

---

[1] *Merriam-Webster's Collegiate Dictionary,* 10th Edition (Springfield, Massachusetts: Merriam-Webster, Inc., 1997).

essay offers a chain of ideas, in which some of the ideas (what we call the **premises**) are meant to provide reasons for believing another idea, the *conclusion*. The premises are usually (and should be) simpler, clearer, and more obvious than the conclusion. And the author should make the connection between the premises and the conclusion clear. Unfortunately, as you will eventually discover, this isn't always the case. The primary task in reading philosophy is to identify the author's premises and conclusion. If you don't catch them all on your first reading, you will understand more on your second reading.

Talk to Your Instructor

If you still do not understand an essay after following all these suggestions, then you should consult your instructor. It may be that the essay you are reading is particularly difficult, complex, or confusing. Your instructor is one of your most important resources. Philosophy instructors, in general, *like* to talk about philosophy and are more than happy to help, clarify, or just chat about your readings.

Reading philosophy can be challenging! But developing this skill will be invaluable to you in many of your other classes, particularly those in the Humanities. The ability to read closely and carefully, to understand not only what the author is trying to prove but also what her reasons are for her conclusions, transfers to many other fields, including economics, physics, medicine, law, and psychology, to name a few. Like any other skill such as playing the piano or working algebra problems, spending time developing this skill will eventually make reading philosophical writing easier. The more you do it, the simpler it gets, and the more enjoyable it becomes.

Calvin and Hobbes   by Bill Watterson

CALVIN AND HOBBES ©1995 Watterson. Reprinted with permission of UNIVERSAL PRESS SYNDICATE. All rights reserved.

3

WRITING FOR UNDERSTANDING

At the most basic level of writing, instructors typically expect two things of a student: *knowledge* of previously learned material (i.e., names, dates, theories, concepts, and principles); and *understanding* of what has been learned. An **understanding essay** is essentially a summary or a paraphrase of an argument. You will often be required to write a summary of a theory on an essay exam, either as a separate question or as part of a question demanding analysis, application, or evaluation. The ability to write a coherent summary of a theory is the first step in understanding it. If you can't summarize an argument or essay in a hundred words or so, then you don't understand it.

Suppose the following passage was part of your weekly reading from John Stuart Mill's *Utilitarianism*:

> The creed which accepts as the foundations of morals "utility" or the "greatest happiness principle" holds that actions are right in proportion as they tend to promote happiness; wrong as they tend to produce the reverse of happiness. By happiness is intended pleasure and the absence of pain; by unhappiness, pain and the privation of pleasure.[1]

If your instructor wants to test your *knowledge* of Mill's greatest happiness principle, then what he is asking for is simple repetition, as in this answer:

> The greatest happiness principle says that an action is right if it produces happiness and wrong if it produces unhappiness. By happiness is intended pleasure, and by unhappiness is intended pain.

[1]John Stuart Mill, *Utilitarianism*, Chapter II, "What Utilitarianism Is" (London: Parker, Son and Bourn, 1863).

12

If, however, your instructor is trying to determine whether you *understand* the greatest happiness principle, then merely repeating Mill's words will not be enough: You must express Mill's principle in your own words. Notice that although the previous answer did not quite use Mill's exact words, still the words and phrases are much too close to Mill's original for the instructor to be certain that you understand what you have read. A better example of understanding would be this:

> According to the greatest happiness principle, what makes an action moral is that it causes happiness (which means pleasure), and what makes an action immoral is that it causes unhappiness (pain). So if it makes people happy, it's right, and if it makes people unhappy, it's wrong.

Aside from some multiple-choice and matching questions on exams, philosophy instructors will rarely ask for mere *knowledge* of a theory, essay, or principle. In fact, even multiple-choice questions often require *understanding* as well. While an instructor will rarely have you write an essay *merely* showing understanding, almost every essay you write will *require* that you show understanding of some theory, essay, or principle. Thus, in order to write *any* kind of philosophical essay, you need to master the understanding essay first.

You show that you understand a theory or essay by using paraphrases and summaries. It is important that you understand the difference.

PARAPHRASING

Paraphrasing a passage means simply to put the ideas and thoughts of an author into your own words. That is, when you paraphrase, you show the meaning of the passage by presenting it in another form—that is, in other words. If your instructor asks you to define a principle, she is asking you to paraphrase the appropriate passage. In the examples above, I paraphrased Mill's Greatest Happiness Principle. Be careful, however, that you don't stick so closely to the author's words, syntax, and sentence structure that you are guilty of plagiarism, or presenting the author's writing—or wording very close to it—as your own. We will discuss plagiarism in depth in Chapter 8. (See the Doonesbury cartoon for an example of what *not* to do.) The first example above commits plagiarism. You must always use your own words, whether on an exam or in an essay, no matter how inelegant they may be compared to the original. This is not only to avoid plagiarism, but also because only in that way can you demonstrate to your instructor that you understand the principle in question.

Consider the following passage from René Descartes's *Meditations on First Philosophy:*

> Several years have now elapsed since I first became aware that I had accepted, even from my youth, many false opinions for true, and that consequently what I afterward based on such principles was highly

DOONESBURY ©1995 G. B. Trudeau. Reprinted with permission of UNIVERSAL PRESS SYNDICATE. All right reserved.

doubtful; and from that time I was convinced of the necessity of undertaking once in my life to rid myself of all the opinions I had adopted, and of commencing anew the work of building from the foundation, if I desired to establish a firm and abiding superstructure in the sciences.[2]

Here is a bad example of a paraphrase of this passage:

Descartes says that he became aware that he had accepted many false opinions as being true, and thus the opinions he built on those false opinions were highly doubtful. He realized that he needed to get rid of all the opinions he had adopted and build a foundation. Otherwise he could not establish anything firm and lasting in the sciences.

This paraphrase is bad because it mimics Descartes's words and syntax much too closely. The following is a better example of paraphrasing. It shows that the writer understands the passage in a way that the earlier example does not.

Descartes says that it has been many years now since he discovered that many of the things he thought were true were actually false. He realized

---

[2]René Descartes, *Meditations on First Philosophy In Which The Existence of God And The Distinction of the Soul from the Body Are Demonstrated*, from *The Method, Meditations and Philosophy of Descartes*, trans. John Veitch (Washington, D.C.: M. Walter Dunne, Publisher, 1901), "Meditation I: Of the Things on Which We May Doubt," p. 219.

that he needed to reject any ideas he had that he could not be absolutely certain about. Otherwise there would be no way to be sure of anything.

Notice that this paraphrase is true to the original—that is, it expresses the same ideas—but it uses words and sentence structure sufficiently different from the original that it is fairly clear that the passage has been understood.

SUMMARIZING

When you are asked to describe or explain an entire theory, argument, or essay, you need to write a **summary.** If you merely paraphrase every sentence, then you will end up with an essay as long as the original. A summary should be considerably shorter than the original. It is not a sentence-by-sentence paraphrase and it does not use the author's words, phrases, or sentence structure. In a summary, you are attempting to explain the essay's major points. This means that you must identify not only the author's *conclusions*, but also his reasons (his *premises*) for those conclusions. If your summary is too long, then you do not understand the essay well enough.

No matter what kind of essay you plan to write, you should write one or more summaries beforehand. Writing a very short summary will help you decide if you understand the argument or theory. If you are writing about a particular argument or theory, write a short (100–200 words) summary of the argument first. Simply passing your eyes over the page and underlining important passages does not guarantee that you understand what you have read. Remember when you summarize a passage or essay that you must identify the reasons an author gives for his views, as well as his conclusion.

Do not begin writing a summary until you have finished reading the entire essay or argument, and don't expect to be able to write a good summary after only one reading. Sometimes earlier passages cannot be completely understood without the connections made in later passages, and sometimes the main point isn't clear until the end of the essay. Be sure you understand what the author is trying to prove or accomplish before you begin your summary. Remember, you need to know more than just his conclusions. You need to be sure that you understand the reasons he gives for those conclusions as well. Getting to this point takes time—lots of patient reading and rereading.

As you read the essay you intend to summarize, jot down what seem to be the major points and premises. Then, when you are ready to begin writing the summary, close your book and write the summary from memory. If you find that you must constantly refer to the essay you are trying to summarize, then you do not yet understand the essay well enough. By not looking at the original essay, you will prevent unintended quoting and plagiarism and will force yourself to rely only on what you actually understand. Continual reference back to the original will probably result in mere paraphrasing of the original. When you paraphrase a passage sentence-by-sentence, you may understand each sentence individually but not the context—how the premises fit together to prove the conclusion.

Premises, remember, are the reasons the author gives for thinking her conclusions are true. The premises are generally simpler and clearer ideas that fit together in a particular way to provide proof or evidence for an idea—the conclusion—that is less obvious and probably less clear. Paraphrase is most often required when you are asked on an essay exam to define a term, principle, or theory. Another use of paraphrase comes in an essay when you are trying to lay out an author's premises and conclusions. You usually need to paraphrase the most important points, rather than simply summarize the whole argument.

The most important question you should ask yourself about any paraphrase or summary is this: Does my paraphrase/summary accurately reflect what the original essay or passage says? You need to be sure that anyone reading your paraphrase/summary will be able to understand the important points made by the author, even though he is unfamiliar with the original. That is, a paraphrase should convey *exactly* the same meaning as the original, although using different words and syntax. A summary should provide a much shorter, but still accurate, rendering of the entire argument or essay.

EXAMPLES

If your instructor asks you to write an "understanding essay," whether on an exam or as an out-of-class assignment, she will most often use one or more of these words: Explain, define, discuss, describe, or summarize. Often a question requiring understanding will begin, "What is . . ." or "What are . . . ." For example, the following are possible essay exam questions or essay topics that require you to understand an essay, principle, or argument:

1. *Explain Hume's reasons for questioning the idea of the self.*

The following is the passage from which your answer would be drawn.

There are some philosophers who imagine we are every moment intimately conscious of what we call our *self;* that we feel its existence and its continuance in existence; and are certain, beyond the evidence of a demonstration, both of its perfect identity and simplicity. . . .

For my part, when I enter most intimately into what I call *myself,* I always stumble on some particular perception or other, of heat or cold, light or shade, love or hatred, pain or pleasure. I never can catch *myself* at any time without a perception, and never can observe any thing but the perception. When my perceptions are removed for any time, as by sound sleep, so long am I insensible of *myself,* and may truly be said not to exist. And were all my perceptions removed by death, and could I neither think, nor feel, nor see, nor love, nor hate, after the dissolution of my body, I should be entirely annihilated, nor do I conceive what is farther requisite to make me a perfect non-entity. If any one, upon serious and unprejudiced reflection, thinks he has a different notion of *himself*, I must confess I can reason no longer with him. All I can allow him is, that he may be in the right as well as I, and that we are essentially different in this particular. He may, perhaps, perceive something simple and continued, which he calls *himself;* though I am certain there is no such principle in me.

But setting aside some metaphysicians of this kind, I may venture to affirm of the rest of mankind, that they are nothing but a bundle or collection of different perceptions, which succeed each other with an inconceivable rapidity, and are in a perpetual flux and movement. . . . The mind is a kind of theatre, where several perceptions successively make their appearance; pass, repass, glide away, and mingle in an infinite variety of postures and situations. There is properly no *simplicity* in it at one time, nor *identity* in different, whatever natural propension we may have to imagine that simplicity and identity. The comparison of the theatre must not mislead us. They are the successive perceptions only, that constitute the mind; nor have we the most distant notion of the place where these scenes are represented, or of the materials, of which it is composed.[3]

So what does the passage mean? This summary answers the essay question:

Hume says that even though people think they have a "self" which is what makes them the same person they were yesterday, last week, last year, and even 10, 20, or 30 years ago, when he looks for his "self" all he finds are perceptions—emotions, thoughts, memories, feelings, etc. What he doesn't find is this "self" which is supposedly the thing that has these perceptions. Hume concludes that he and the rest of mankind are simply "bundles of perceptions." That is, our "self" is just the sum total of our perceptions. So when we are asleep or unconscious and are not conscious of perceptions, then our "self" does not exist.

This is a good summary because it does not mimic Hume's words or sentence structure too closely and it accurately reflects his main points in the passage.

2. Why does Descartes think we should doubt what we know, and what are his three reasons for doubting?

Here are the appropriate passages:

Several years have now elapsed since I first became aware that I had accepted, even from my youth, many false opinions for true, and that consequently what I afterward based on such principles was highly

---

[3]David Hume, *A Treatise of Human Nature*, "Book I, Part IV, Of Personal Identity" (London: J.M. Dent & Sons LTD, 1911), pp. 238–40.

doubtful; and from that time I was convinced of the necessity of undertaking once in my life to rid myself of all the opinions I had adopted,
and of commencing anew the work of building from the foundation, if
I desired to establish a firm and abiding superstructure in the sciences
. . . . I will at length apply myself earnestly and freely to the general
overthrow of all my former opinions. But, to this end, it will not be necessary for me to show that the whole of these are false—a point, perhaps, which I shall never reach; but as even now my reason convinces
me that I ought not the less carefully to withhold belief from what is not
entirely certain and indubitable, than from what is manifestly false, it
will be sufficient to justify the rejection of the whole if I shall find in
each some ground for doubt. Nor for this purpose will it be necessary
even to deal with each belief individually, which would be truly an end-
less labor; but as the removal from below of the foundation necessarily
involves the downfall of the whole edifice, I will at once approach the
criticism of the principles on which all my former beliefs rested.

   All that I have, up to this moment, accepted as possessed of the
highest truth and certainty, I received either from or through the senses.
I observed, however, that these sometimes misled us; and it is the part
of prudence not to place absolute confidence in that by which we have
even once been deceived.

   But, it may be said, perhaps, that, although the senses occasionally
mislead us respecting minute objects, and such as are so far removed
from us as to be beyond the reach of close observation, there are yet
many other of their informations (presentations), of the truth of which it
is manifestly impossible to doubt; as for example, that I am in this place,
seated by the fire, clothed in a winter dressing gown, that I hold in my
hands this piece of paper, with other intimations of the same nature. . . .

   Though this be true, I must nevertheless here consider that I am a
man, and that, consequently, I am in the habit of sleeping, and representing to myself in dreams those same things, or even sometimes
others less probable. . . . How often have I dreamt that I was in these
familiar circumstances, that I was dressed, and occupied this place by
the fire, when I was lying undressed in bed? At the present moment,
however, I certainly look upon this paper with eyes wide awake; the
head which I now move is not asleep; I extend this hand consciously
and with express purpose, and I perceive it; the occurrences in sleep are
not so distinct as all this. But I cannot forget that, at other times I have
been deceived in sleep by similar illusions; and, attentively considering
those cases, I perceive so clearly that there exist no certain marks by
which the state of waking can ever be distinguished from sleep, that I
feel greatly astonished; and in amazement I almost persuade myself
that I am now dreaming.

   Let us suppose, then, that we are dreaming, and that all these partic-
ulars—namely the opening of the eyes, the motion of the head, the forth-
putting of the hands—are merely illusions; and even that we really possess neither an entire body nor hands such as we see. Nevertheless . . .

whether I am awake or dreaming, it remains true that two and three make five, and that a square has but four sides; nor does it seem possible that truths so apparent can ever fall under a suspicion of falsity [or incertitude].

Nevertheless, the belief that there is a God who is all powerful, and who created me, such as I am, has, for a long time, obtained steady possession of my mind. How, then, do I know that he has not arranged that there should be neither earth, nor sky, nor any extended thing, nor figure, nor magnitude, nor place, providing at the same time, however, for [the rise in me of the perceptions of all these objects, and] the persuasion that these do not exist otherwise than as I perceive them? And further . . . how do I know that I am not deceived each time I add together two and three, or number the sides of a square, or form some judgement still more simple, if more simple indeed can be imagined? But perhaps Deity has not been willing that I should be thus deceived, for he is said to be supremely good. . . .

I will suppose, then, not that Deity, who is sovereignly good and the foundation of truth, but that some malignant demon, who is at once exceedingly potent and deceitful, has employed all his artifice to deceive me; I will suppose that the sky, the air, the earth, colors, figures, sounds, and all external things, are nothing better than the illusions of dreams, by means of which this being has laid snares for my credulity; I will consider myself as without hands, eyes, flesh, blood, or any of the senses, and as falsely believing that I am possessed of these; I will continue resolutely fixed in this belief, and if indeed by this means it be not in my power to arrive at the knowledge of truth, I shall at least do what is in my power, viz [suspend judgment], and guard with settled purpose against giving assent to what is false, and being imposed upon by this deceiver, whatever be his power and artifice.[4]

This essay question asks, Why does Descartes think we should doubt what we know, and what are his three reasons for doubting? Here is a good summary:

Descartes thinks that unless we can be absolutely certain that something is true, then we should not believe it. He thinks that most of what we think we know isn't true, or at least might not be, because we can't be sure about even the most basic things. His first reason for doubting is that most of what we know we have learned through our senses, and sometimes our senses are wrong (like an optical illusion or an echo). His second reason for doubting is that at least sometimes we cannot be sure whether we are dreaming or awake, so it is always possible that what we think we are experiencing is just a dream. And finally, Descartes's third reason for doubting is that there may be an evil genius who is constantly deceiving us about our senses, our dreams, or even about $1 + 1 = 2$.

[4]Descartes, *Mediations on First Philosophy*, pp. 219–24.

Descartes thinks that these three reasons for doubting mean that there is nothing that we can be sure of, and thus we must doubt everything we think we know.

Again, notice that this answer accurately summarizes the original passage, but does not plagiarize by sticking too closely to Descartes's words or syntax.

3. *Why does Hume say that we should be skeptical of miracles?*

Here are the appropriate passages:

> A miracle is a violation of the laws of nature; and as a firm and unalterable experience has established these laws, the proof against a miracle, from the very nature of the fact, is as entire as any argument from experience can possibly be imagined. Why is it more than probable, that all men must die; that lead cannot, of itself, remain suspended in the air; that fire consumes wood, and is extinguished by water; unless it be, that these events are found agreeable to the laws of nature, and there is required a violation of these laws, or in other words, a miracle to prevent them? Nothing is esteemed a miracle, if it ever happen in the common course of nature. It is no miracle that a man, seemingly in good health, should die on a sudden: because such a kind of death, though more unusual than any other, has yet been frequently observed to happen. But it is a miracle, that a dead man should come to life; because that has never been observed in any age or country. There must, therefore, be a uniform experience against every miraculous event, otherwise the event would not merit that appellation. And as a uniform experience amounts to a proof, there is here a direct and full *proof*, from the nature of the fact, against the existence of any miracle; nor can such a proof be destroyed, or the miracle rendered credible, but by an opposite proof, which is superior.
>
> The plain consequence is (and it is a general maxim worthy of our attention), 'That no testimony is sufficient to establish a miracle, unless the testimony be of such a kind, that its falsehood would be more miraculous, than the fact, which it endeavours to establish'. . . . When anyone tells me, that he saw a dead man restored to life, I immediately consider with myself, whether it be more probable, that this person should either deceive or be deceived, or that the fact, which he relates, should really have happened. I weigh the one miracle against the other; and according to the superiority, which I discover, I pronounce my decision, and always reject the greater miracle. If the falsehood of his testimony would be more miraculous, than the even which he relates; then, and not till then, can he pretend to command my belief or opinion.[5]

---

[5]David Hume, *Enquiries concerning Human Understanding and concerning the Principles of Morals*, 2nd ed., eds. L.A. Selby-Bigge and P.H. Nidditch (Oxford: Oxford University Press, 1902), pp. 114–16.

Why does Hume say that we should be skeptical of miracles? Here is a good response:

> Hume says that a law of nature is something that many people have observed on many occasions and have never seen violated, so that we call it a "law." A miracle, by definition, is a violation of a law of nature (like returning from the dead, or defying gravity). When someone tells us about a miracle, we have to weigh one person's claim about what he says he saw, with a universal claim about the corresponding law of nature. Then we should ask ourselves which would be the greater miracle, that the witness or witnesses are mistaken or lying, or that all the witnesses to the law of nature are mistaken or lying. Since it would be a greater miracle if all the witnesses to the law of nature were wrong, Hume clearly thinks that no evidence, regardless of how reliable the witnesses, will ever be enough to say that a miracle occurred.

When writing a summary, remember to ask yourself: Does my summary accurately reflect what the original essay or passage says? If not, try again. Be sure that you do not just paraphrase, or, worst of all, plagiarize, the author's own sentences. An instructor requests a summary when she wants to know whether you understand an essay or passage. Mere paraphrase or quotation does not show that you understand the argument.

4

WRITING FOR APPLICATION

Writing what I call an **application essay** is more difficult than merely knowing and understanding the theory that you are writing about. Of course, you have to understand the theory *first* (which is why you should master the understanding essay described in Chapter 3 first). To write an application essay, you need to take what you have learned in another context and apply it to a new situation.

This is a favorite type of essay exam question for many professors—particularly when the questions are about ethical theories. For example, Kant has a famous ethical dilemma (which I call his "homicidal maniac case") about a murderer who comes knocking at your door wanting to know where his victim is.[1] Unbeknownst to the homicidal maniac, just moments before, his victim (a friend of yours) came to you and asked if he could hide in your basement. You said yes. The victim is now in the basement, and the homicidal maniac asks you where the victim is. The dilemma is this: Should you tell the truth to the homicidal maniac? For various reasons (which I won't get into here), Kant's ethical theory states very clearly that you should *not* tell a lie, you have a duty to tell the truth always, and thus you must tell the homicidal maniac that his victim is in your basement. If he goes downstairs and kills the victim, well, Kant says, it isn't your fault. You did the right thing (telling the truth) and you aren't responsible if doing your duty leads to bad consequences.

Now, many ethical theorists don't agree with Kant's conclusion. So a typical application question might ask you to *apply* another ethical theory to this example from Kant. For instance:

---

[1] Immanuel Kant, "On a Supposed Right to Tell Lies from Benevolent Motives," 1797, in *Critique of Practical Reason and Other Writings in Moral Philosophy*, trans. Lewis White Beck (Chicago: University of Chicago Press, 1949).

> What is Mill's principle of utility? Using Kant's example of whether you should tell the truth to a murderer about the location of his victim, explain what you think Mill would say you should do, and why.

Mill never wrote about this example, so you don't *know* what the correct answer is here, and no amount of studying your text will tell you. However, even though you can't be sure what Mill would say, if you understand his principle of utility, you should be able to make a pretty good guess as to what his answer would be to Kant's dilemma.

If this were an essay exam question, the following would be a sample answer:

> Mill's principle of utility states that an action is right if it leads to happiness and wrong if it leads to unhappiness. Mill defines happiness as pleasure and the absence of pain. He also says that everybody's happiness counts, and that short-term and long-term happiness both have to be considered.
>
> In the case of Kant's homicidal maniac, I think Mill would say that you should lie to the homicidal maniac. I guess it would probably make the homicidal maniac unhappy if you tell him a lie, because then he can't kill his victim. However, that is a small amount of unhappiness for one person, versus a large amount of unhappiness for at least two if you tell the truth. You are going to be unhappy when the homicidal maniac kills your friend, and your friend is going to be really unhappy if he gets killed. Also your friend's family is going to be unhappy. And in the long run, the maniac may be unhappy if he gets caught and goes to jail. So the most happiness for the most number of people would be if you lie to the maniac.

Notice that the writer of this essay *first* states the principle of utility in her own words (that is, she does not merely quote Mill's words), and *then* she applies it to a new situation and comes up with an answer. Notice also that she doesn't merely say, "Mill would say tell the lie." She explains why he would say that—how his theory leads to that conclusion.

Here's another sample question:

> What do you think Locke would say about the identity of a person with amnesia? That is, is she the same person she was before she got amnesia?

Again, you don't *know* what Locke's answer to this question would be. The best you can do is predict, using his theory, what his answer would be. Even though the question doesn't explicitly ask for a summary of Locke's theory, you need to first explain the theory, and then explain why that theory leads to your answer. Here is a sample answer:

> According to Locke, what makes me the same person I was yesterday and last week and last year, is the fact that I can remember being that person. So my memory is what makes me, me. If this is true, then a person with

total amnesia would not be the same person she was before she got amnesia. If she can't remember being that person, then the person she is now is a different person. If she has partial amnesia, then she is the same person for the times she can remember, but a different person from the times she can't remember.

Another sample question and answer:

Question: What are the four Aristotelian causes of a piece of chocolate cake?

Answer: Aristotle says that everything has four causes: efficient, material, formal, and final. The material cause is what the thing is made of. The formal cause is the form of the thing (for example, a chair, a baseball, a cake). The final cause is the purpose of the thing. The efficient cause is what we usually mean by cause—the creator or whatever. The material cause of the piece of chocolate cake is the flour, sugar, chocolate, etc. that the cake is made of. The efficient cause is the person who baked the cake. The formal cause is the "cake-like" shape of it (three layer, or wedding cake, or whatever). That is, the formal cause is why the flour, sugar, and chocolate come together to make a cake instead of a cookie or a pie or something else. The final cause, the purpose, is to be eaten and to be enjoyed and to nourish a human being.

These are fairly simple examples of applying something you already know to a new and different situation. Of course, application essays can be much more complicated. An ethics instructor, for example, might ask you to choose a moral theory and then write a paper from that standpoint about euthanasia or capital punishment. Entire books have been written doing that kind of thing. A few that come to mind are *Feminist Interpretations of Immanuel Kant,*[2] which applies feminism to Kant's philosophy; Peter Singer's *Practical Ethics,*[3] which is an extended application of utilitarianism to various moral problems; and Glen McGee's *The Perfect Baby,*[4] which applies pragmatism to various problems in genetics.

USING EXAMPLES

Another type of application essay or exam question asks you to provide **examples**. Any time you are asked to "give an example of," "show how," "demonstrate," or "illustrate," you are being asked to apply some theory or principle to a new situation. For example:

---

[2]Robin May Schott, ed., *Feminist Interpretations of Immanuel Kant (Re-Reading the Canon)* (University Park, PA: Pennsylvania State University Press, 1997).
[3]Peter Singer, *Practical Ethics* (New York: Cambridge University Press, 1979).
[4]Glenn McGee, *The Perfect Baby: A Pragmatic Approach to Genetics* (Lanham, MD: Rowman & Littlefield Publishers, Inc., 1997).

Explain Kant's distinction between perfect and imperfect duties. Provide examples of each.

Here's a sample answer:

Kant says that we have perfect and imperfect duties. A perfect duty is one which we must always do. It is something I have a duty to do which some other person has a right to expect me to do. For example, I have a perfect duty to tell the truth to people, since everyone has a right to be told the truth by me. An imperfect duty is one that I have to do, but there isn't any one person you can point to who has a right to it. For example, Kant says that I have a duty to give to charity. It's only an imperfect duty because although I have to give to charity, I don't have to give it to any one in particular. No specific person or charity has a right to my charity.

A good use of an example comes from James Rachels. Rachels tries to argue that killing someone and letting someone die are *morally* equivalent. (This is in reference to a question about euthanasia.) Many people feel that allowing a patient to die by not treating her (for example, when a cancer patient refuses to continue chemotherapy treatments) is morally acceptable, while giving that same patient a lethal injection (so that she could die quickly and painlessly) is killing—and therefore is morally wrong. Rachels suggests that you can't make that kind of distinction between killing and letting someone die, and he gives the following example:[5]

Smith has a six-year-old cousin who is fabulously wealthy. If the cousin dies, Smith is his heir and will inherit all the money. So one evening while the cousin is taking a bath, Smith sneaks into the bathroom and holds the child's head under water until he drowns.

Smith, clearly, has done something very wrong here. Now consider Jones's situation:

Jones also has a six-year-old cousin who is fabulously wealthy. If the cousin dies, Jones is his heir and will inherit all the money. So one evening while the cousin is taking a bath, Jones goes into the bathroom, intending to drown the cousin. However, as Jones walks in the bathroom door, the cousin slips in the tub, hits his head and is knocked unconscious, and falls face down in the water. Jones stands in the doorway and watches as the cousin drowns.

Is there any morally relevant difference between what Smith and Jones did? Most people would say no. Both of them are responsible (morally and legally) for the death of the cousin. But Smith "killed" his cousin, while Jones only "let his cousin die." Does it matter? If not, then Rachels's example is a good one to show why there is no moral distinction.

---

[5]Paraphrased from James Rachels, "Active and Passive Euthanasia," *New England Journal of Medicine* 292, no. 2 (January 9, 1975), pp. 78–80.

USING COUNTER-EXAMPLES

Another type of example you may be asked to provide in an application essay or exam is a **counter-example**—an example meant to show that a theory or principle is incorrect. Many people consider Kant's homicidal maniac case to be a counter-example to his moral theory. Because they think that it is obviously true that you should lie to a maniac in order to save a life, the fact that Kant's theory says that you should not lie means that Kant's theory must be wrong. According to Bernard Williams, the following case provides a counter-example to utilitarianism:

> You find yourself in the central square of a small South American village. Tied up against the wall is a row of 20 people. The captain in charge explains that the 20 villagers are a random group of the inhabitants who, after recent acts of protest against the government, are just about to be killed to remind other protestors of the advantages of not protesting. However, the captain is happy to offer you a guest's privilege of killing one of the people yourself. If you accept, the others will be let off. Of course, if you refuse, then the men with the guns will do what they were about to do when you arrived and kill them all. You wonder whether if you got hold of a gun, you could kill the captain and the rest of the soldiers, but it is quite clear from the set-up that nothing of the kind is going to work: Any attempt at that sort of thing will mean that all 20 of the villagers will be killed and so will you. The people against the wall and the other villagers understand the situation and are obviously begging you to accept. What should you do?[6]

A utilitarian (that is, a person who agrees with the principle of utility), would say that you should shoot the one villager to save the 19 others. Since these people and the other villagers (including their families, presumably) understand and are in favor of you shooting one of them, it seems clear that more people will be happy if you shoot one, rather than let the soldiers kill 20. However, Williams suggests that you might feel very strongly that it would be wrong for you to shoot one of the villagers (since he is, probably, an innocent victim, he hasn't harmed you, and thus it is cold-blooded murder), and thus utilitarianism must be wrong. Of course, many utilitarians would disagree with Williams. That is, some utilitarians say, "Yes, the thing that would make the most people happy would be for me to shoot one, and therefore that would be the right thing to do." Other utilitarians suggest that, in fact, shooting one *won't* make the most people happy—and go on to explain. In either case, this example should have taught you a valuable lesson about counter-examples. A good counter-example must be *obviously*

---

[6]Slightly revised version of the example from Bernard Williams, "A Critique of Utilitarianism," in *Utilitarianism: For and Against,* by Bernard Williams and J. J. C. Smart (New York: Cambridge University Press, 1973), pp. 98–99.

wrong. So neither of the two examples I have just given are going to be very satisfying counter-examples.

On the other hand, the following may offers a fair example of why utilitarianism isn't correct (and is thus a good counter-example):

> Suppose Joe comes into the hospital unconscious. He has been hit by a car and has been knocked unconscious. He has a broken arm but no other injuries and is otherwise very healthy. At the time Joe is brought into the hospital, there are several people who are waiting for transplant organs. Sue needs a heart, Jay and Julie need kidneys, Helen needs a liver, and Lisa needs a lung. Without a transplant, each of these people will die. All of these people have families and friends who desperately want them to live. Joe, on the other hand, is an orphan with few friends. What would a utilitarian say you should do?

With the information we've been given, a utilitarian would say that the action that will lead to the most happiness for the most people would be to sacrifice Joe for his organs. Most people, even many utilitarians, would not agree. So this is a good counter-example to utilitarianism. And, if you are trying to show that Kant's moral theory is better than utilitarianism, this would be a good example for why Kant is right. Since Kant's theory would suggest that you cannot sacrifice one innocent person (even if he is an orphan) to save five other lives, this provides a good example supporting Kant's theory.

CONCLUDING REMARKS

The key to providing either examples or counter-examples is to be sure that they very clearly show what you want. A good counter-example must show, to the satisfaction of most people anyway, that the theory is false. That is, it must be pretty clear that the consequences of accepting the theory are unacceptable. A good example, on the other hand, needs to clearly illustrate the theory or principle in question. Using Kant's homicidal maniac case to show why his moral theory is correct is probably a bad idea, since many people would consider it a counter-example.

Even if you aren't asked to give an example or a counter-example, it is often wise to do so, particularly on essay exams. Examples and counter-examples are useful in making a theory or principle clearer and more understandable. Applying a theory or principle to new situations by creating examples shows a higher level of understanding than just explaining the theory, in the same way that (as I showed in the last chapter) summarizing a theory in your own words shows a higher level of understanding than merely repeating or quoting the author's original words.

5

WRITING FOR ANALYSIS

When your instructor asks you to provide an **analysis** of an essay, argument, or theory, he is not merely asking you to explain what the author is saying. To analyze an argument, you must not only understand the *content* of the argument, but you should also understand its *structure*. You must be able to break the argument down into its component parts and recognize the relationship between those parts. This means that you must not only understand each of the separate parts of the argument or theory, but you need to determine the connections and interactions between those parts. In order to help you write for analysis, this chapter will show you how to distinguish conclusions from the premises that support them, facts from opinions, necessary from probable conclusions, and assumptions from logical conclusions. In addition, you will learn to detect unstated assumptions, logical fallacies, and emotive language.

ARGUMENTS

An **argument,** remember, is a set of statements, one of which is the conclusion and the rest of which are the premises. The premises are supposed to give you reasons, evidence, or justification for believing that the conclusion is true. The premises are the statements the author uses to provide reasons for thinking the conclusion is true. If the argument is a good one, then the truth of the premises will give you good reasons for believing that the conclusion is true. If the argument is a bad one, then it will not give you reason to believe the truth of the conclusion. Thus, when you think about an argument, you need to ask yourself: What is the author trying to convince me of? What position is he trying to defend? This is the conclusion. The rest of the essay explains the connections between the premises and the con-clusion, in order to establish why the premises are true and possibly to give examples to show that the argument is valid or strong.

There are two kinds of arguments: deductive and inductive. A **deduc-tive argument** is one in which, if the argument is a good one, the premises guarantee the truth of the conclusion. For example, the following is a deductive argument:

(P1—premise 1) All dogs are animals.

(P2—premise 2) Ralph is a dog.

Therefore, (C—conclusion) Ralph is an animal.

Notice that if the first two statements are true (that is, that Ralph really is a dog and is not a cat or a fish or something else, and if, in fact, all dogs really are animals), then it must be the case that Ralph is an animal. The conclusion "Ralph is an animal" cannot be false if the premises are true.

In a good **inductive argument,** on the other hand, the truth of the premises only makes it *probable* that the conclusion is true. For example:

(P1) Most medical doctors are wealthy.

(P2) Dr. Gonzalez is a medical doctor.

Therefore, (C) Dr. Gonzalez is probably wealthy.

Notice that even if the premises are true—most doctors *are* wealthy and Dr. Gonzalez *is* a medical doctor—it still might not be true that Dr. Gonzalez is wealthy. P1 only claims that *most* doctors are wealthy, implying that some doctors are not. And Dr. Gonzalez may be one of the few who is not wealthy. So while we can be reasonably sure that Dr. Gonzalez is wealthy, we can't be absolutely positive in the same way we were absolutely positive that Ralph was an animal in the last example.

It is important that you understand the difference between deductive and inductive arguments, not only so that you can recognize them when you see them, but also so that you don't make the mistake of claiming that you have proven more than you really have. If an argument is inductive, then the best that can be said is that the conclusion is *probably* true. If you, or any other author, claim to have certainly proven your conclusion, the argument had better be deductive.

Of course, not all deductive or inductive arguments are good argu-ments. The two previous examples are good examples, but others aren't. There are two ways an argument can go "bad." First, *one or more of the premises may not be true.* In the first example above, if Ralph is something else and not a dog, then we can't be sure that he is an animal. (Maybe Ralph is my car.) Second, an argument can go wrong if something is wrong with its structure or form. For instance, consider the following argument:

(P1) If fetuses are people, then it is wrong to kill them.

(P2) Fetuses are not people.

Therefore, (C) it is not wrong to kill fetuses.

What's wrong with this argument? At first sight, maybe nothing. However, consider the following argument, which structurally is exactly the same:

(P1) If Ralph is a dog, then Ralph is an animal.

(P2) Ralph is not a dog.

Therefore, (C) Ralph is not an animal.

It is possible for both P1 and P2 to be true, but for C to be false. How? What if Ralph is a fish? P2 is true, since Ralph is not a dog. P1 is also true. Since all dogs are animals, then if Ralph was a dog, he would also be an animal. But it is not true that (C) Ralph is not an animal—fish are animals too! Since a good deductive argument is one in which the truth of the premises is supposed to guarantee the truth of the conclusion, this is not a good deductive argument. In fact, it is what we call an *invalid* argument. Validity has to do with the structure of the argument, not the content of the statements. What is wrong with these two arguments is *not* that any or all of the statements are false. What is wrong is that the conclusions don't follow from the premises. If the true premises in the argument about Ralph do not guarantee the truth of the conclusion, then even if the premises in the fetus argument are true, you can't be sure the conclusion is true—no matter how convincing you may have found it at first.

If an argument is valid and it has true premises, then it is called a *sound* argument. When I spoke of "good" arguments, these are the kind I meant— the premises are true, the form is valid, and thus we are guaranteed that the conclusion is also true. Trying to explain how to distinguish valid from invalid arguments is well beyond the scope of this book (see Appendix B for a list of books that address these issues). However, just being aware of the necessity of having both a valid argument and true premises will put you way ahead of the game.

Good inductive arguments are very similar to good deductive arguments. An inductive argument, remember, is one in which, if the premises are true, then the conclusion is probably true. Suppose I present the following argument:

(P1) Most professors are rich.

(P2) Dr. Gildrie is a professor.

Therefore (C) Dr. Gildrie is probably rich.

This is what we call a *strong* inductive argument. *If* the premises are true, then the conclusion is also probably true. However, this argument suffers from a false premise. In fact, it isn't true that most professors are rich.

Like a deductive argument, an inductive argument may have true premises but still not be a good argument. For example:

(P) I talked to 3 of my 126 students, and every one said I was the best teacher at the school.

Therefore, (C) I must be the best teacher at the school.

Notice that I talked to only 3 out of 126 students. That probably isn't very good evidence that I am the best teacher at the school. The premises in an inductive argument are supposed to give me good reasons for thinking the conclusion is probably true, and that just isn't the case here. Perhaps if I talked to 100 of the 126 students, or even 80 or 90 of them, then I might have a better reason for thinking I am the best teacher at the school. However, the fact that 3 students think I'm wonderful doesn't imply that they *all* do. This is what we call a *weak* inductive argument. The premises don't provide the necessary support for the conclusion. A good inductive argument—one in which not only are the premises true, but they also provide adequate support for thinking the conclusion is true—is called a *cogent* argument.

Again, teaching you everything you need to know in order to identify cogent arguments is beyond the scope of this book, but just be aware that, like deductive arguments, inductive arguments can have false premises or a weak form or both. But notice that just because an argument has one of these flaws, it isn't necessarily true that it has both flaws. Remember this example:

(P1) All dogs are animals.

(P2) Ralph is a dog.

Therefore, (C) Ralph is an animal.

If Ralph is a fish, then P2 is false, but the conclusion is true. Similarly, in the following example:

(P1) All dogs are animals.

(P2) Ralph is not a dog.

Therefore, (C) Ralph is not an animal.

If Ralph is my car, then the premises and the conclusion are true, but the argument has an invalid form and thus is not a good argument.

The moral of all this is that when you want to analyze an argument, you need to consider two things. First, if all the premises were true, would they give you good reason to think that the conclusion is true? Second, are all the premises true? To answer the first question, you either need to take a logic course or try to manage with the information I have given you here. In the second case, you need to consult the appropriate factual material. That is, in order to know if the premises of the previous argument are true, you need to (1) find out if all dogs are animals by consulting a biology book, your own memory, or your own common sense, and (2) take a look at Ralph to see if he is a dog or not.

ANALYZING ARGUMENTS

When you approach an argument or theory in order to analyze it, you must follow some very simple steps.

Identify the Main Conclusion

Each essay you read is probably trying to establish and convince you of one thing and one thing only. Ask yourself, What is the author's *main* point? He may have several secondary points, but the one main point should be pretty clear. (In fact, it is sometimes indicated in the title of the essay.) Probably it will be indicated in the first paragraph or two of the essay.

Identify the Premises

What supporting reasons does the author present for thinking his main point is true? Sometimes an author has hidden assumptions that may or may not be obvious to you. For example, if I say:

(P1) Ralph is a dog;

Therefore, (C) Ralph is an animal,

I have a hidden assumption (that all dogs are animals) and I am just assuming that you already know that. Some of these hidden assumptions—or unstated premises—will be common knowledge. However, some will not. You need to be sure that you make explicit anything that the author is assuming to be true that is crucial to his argument.

For example, suppose the author says:

(P1) The Bible says abortion is wrong.

Therefore, (C) abortion is wrong.

There are several unstated premises here. First of all, the speaker is assuming that the Bible is the word of God and thus what it says is true. This assumption implies that God exists, which many people don't believe. Whether the argument is good or bad isn't my point here. My point is simply that understanding this argument requires that you discover any unstated premises it relies on.

Clarify Any Ambiguous Words or Phrases

Philosophers often use words in a more technical way than they are used in common speech. So, for instance, an author who discusses "democracy" or "causation," or uses the words "determined" or "certain," may not mean what you think she means. Clarifying the meaning of an author's terms may involve consulting a philosophy dictionary or an encyclopedia of philosophy (see Appendix B). In any case, if you are not clear about what her words mean, you can never hope to be clear about what her argument means. At this point, you need to determine if the premises are true. You can't do that if you don't understand the words used in them.

Determine the Structure or Form of the Argument

Is the argument deductive or inductive? How do the premises fit together with the conclusion in order to prove the conclusion is true? Does the argument seem to be valid or strong? At this point, you need to give the author every benefit of the doubt that you can. That is, when you reconstruct his argument, add any assumptions needed to make it work, and put it into the best form possible. If on one reading of the argument it is obviously wrong and on another it is at least plausible, assume the second reading is the more accurate one. Determining its structure is the hardest part of analyzing an argument. Later in the chapter I will give you examples to show how this is done.

Watch for Emotional Language

Many people rely on **emotional language** in order to persuade you not to look too carefully at their arguments. Watch out for name calling, stereotypes, inflammatory language, and impassioned rhetoric that try to persuade you to adopt a conclusion for which sufficient proof has not been offered. Emotionally charged language is often used to persuade and convince the reader to accept a conclusion, without the arguer having to provide actual reasons or evidence to support that conclusion.

Check to See If There Are Any Fallacies Involved

A **fallacy** is a mistake made in an argument that *seems* correct but really isn't, often because of ambiguities in grammar or the meanings of words or because our inclination is to be convinced by reasons that are not good reasons. The fetus argument I gave earlier committed a formal fallacy. **Formal fallacies** have to do with the form or structure of the argument. An **informal fallacy** occurs when the form of the argument is valid or strong and the premises seem to be true, but the conclusion is (sometimes obviously) false, demonstrating that something has gone wrong in the argument. Checking for fallacies is so important that I will discuss it at length.

The False Dilemma Fallacy   An author is guilty of a **false dilemma fallacy** when he draws a conclusion based on only two alternatives but there are other possibilities. Any time an author claims that there are only two alternatives, be very sure that there really *are* only two alternatives. If there is at least one more possibility, then the author has probably committed the false dilemma fallacy.

Consider the following passage from Plato's *Apology*. In this passage, Socrates is trying to explain to the Athenian jury why their sentencing him to death is not a bad thing:

> Let us reflect in another way, and we shall see that there is great reason to hope that death is a good, for one of two things: either death is a state of nothingness and utter unconsciousness, or, as men say, there is a change and migration of the soul from this world to another. Now if you suppose that there is no consciousness, but a sleep like the sleep of him who is undisturbed even by the sight of dreams, death will be an unspeakable gain. For if a person were to select the night in which his sleep was undisturbed even by dreams, and were to compare with this the other days and nights of his life, and then were to tell us how many days and nights he had passed in the course of his life better and more pleasantly than this one, I think that any man, I will not say a private man, but even the great king [of Persia], will not find many such days or nights, when compared with the others. Now if death is like this, I say that to die is gain; for eternity is then only a single night. But if death is the journey to another place, and there, as men say, all the dead are, what good, O my friends and judges, can be greater than this? If indeed when the pilgrim arrives in the world below, he is delivered from the professors of justice in this world, and finds the true judges who are said to give judgment there, Minos and Rhadamanthus and Aeacus and Triptolemus, and other sons of God who were righteous in their own life, that pilgrimage will be worth making. What would not a man give if he might converse with Orpheus and Musaeus and Hesiod and Homer? Nay, if this be true, let me die again and again. I, too, shall have a wonderful interest in a place where I can converse with Palamedes, and Ajax the son of Telamon, and other heroes of old, who have suffered death through an unjust judgment; and there will be no small pleasure, as I think, in comparing my own sufferings with theirs. Above all, I shall be able to continue my search into true and false knowledge; as in this world, so also in that; I shall find out who is wise, and who pretends to be wise, and is not. What would not a man give, O judges, to be able to examine the leader of the great Trojan expedition; or Odysseus or Sisyphus, or numberless others, men and women too! What infinite delight would there be in conversing with them and asking them questions! For in that world they do not put a man to death for this; certainly not. For besides being happier in that world than in this, they will be immortal, if what is said is true.[1]

Socrates has committed the false dilemma fallacy. His argument looks like this:

[1]Plato, *Apology*, trans. Benjamin Jowett, in *The Greek Classics: Volume Four* (New York: Vincent Parke and Company, 1909), pp. 123–25.

(P1) Either death is nothing (like falling asleep and never waking up), or else death is going on to a better place.

(P2) If death is nothing, then there is no reason to fear it.

(P3) If death is going on to a better place, then there is no reason to fear it.

Therefore, (C) there is no reason to fear death.

This argument is *valid*—that is, if all the premises are true, then the conclusion must also be true. However, the first premise is not true, because Socrates implies that there are only two options: Either death is nothing, or else it is going on to a better place. In fact, it is possible that there is at least one more option—that death might be going on to a *worse* place (like the Judeo-Christian hell). If the third option is true, then death *is* something to fear, and thus Socrates's argument doesn't work. Remember, when an author commits a fallacy, it indicates that something is wrong with his argument, and thus you have no assurance that his conclusion is true.

The Appeal to Unqualified Authority Fallacy   Another common fallacy (which you are less likely to find in the essays you read for class than you are in your own essays) is the fallacy of **appeal to unqualified authority.** An appeal to authority occurs when you say, Such-and-such is true, because so-and-so said it. This can be legitimate in certain contexts. For example, if an argument depends upon a fact about astronomy, saying that Carl Sagan said it is true is probably justified. In the same way, if a premise makes a particular claim about when the fetus develops its central nervous system, then appealing to a respected child development expert or text is legitimate. On the other hand, an appeal to authority is only as good as the believability of the source. If your family doctor tells you that something is true about astronomy, you may not have good reason to believe that it is true. On the other hand, if Carl Sagan tells you that something is true about the development of the fetus, his saying so probably isn't a good reason to think it is true either. Thus people can be authorities in some areas but not in others. However, keep in mind that in philosophy, quoting an authority usually doesn't do any good. Just because Immanuel Kant claims something is true about philosophy doesn't necessarily make it so—despite the fact that Kant is a famous, well-respected philosopher. Philosophical questions are so complex and so often uncertain that we don't usually consider anyone an authority. In philosophy, the *argument* is what is important, not what someone famous thought about the argument.

The False Cause Fallacy   Another common fallacy is the fallacy of **false cause.** False cause involves claiming that one thing caused something else, when in fact it didn't. Sometimes the false cause is just something that happened at the same time. For example, consider the following argument:

(P1) Every time the cheerleaders wear blue ribbons in their hair, the football team wins.

(P2) We want the football team to win tonight's game.

Therefore, (C) the cheerleaders should wear blue ribbons in their hair tonight.

Obviously, the blue ribbons didn't *cause* the football team to win, but the argument implies that they did. Usually the problem is not that the supposed cause is not relevant to the effect, but that we claim it to be the only cause, when in fact it may be one of many. For example:

(P1) Teachers' salaries have been getting lower in terms of buying power every year for the past 10 years.

(P2) Students' SAT scores have been getting lower every year for the past 10 years.

Therefore, (C) if we raise teachers' salaries, then students will get higher scores on the SAT.

While it is possible that one reason students don't score well on the SAT is because their teachers are not well paid, it is not at all obvious (and probably isn't true) that teachers' low salaries are the *sole cause* of students' low scores.

The Is/Ought Fallacy   When an author claims that something ought to be the case simply because it is the case, he has committed one form of the **is/ought fallacy.** Some critics claim that Mill commits this fallacy in his book *Utilitarianism*. Here are two passages to illustrate:

No reason can be given why the general happiness is desirable, except that each person, so far as he believes it to be attainable, desires his own happiness. . . .

If human nature is so constituted as to desire nothing which is not either a part of happiness or a means of happiness—we can have no other proof, and we require no other, that these are the only things desirable. If so, happiness is the sole end of human action, and the promotion of it the test by which to judge of all human conduct; from whence it necessarily follows that it must be the criterion of morality, since a part is included in the whole.[2]

In the first passage, Mill claims that everyone desires happiness (which is probably true). However, he goes on in the second passage to conclude that since everyone *does* desire happiness, they *ought* to desire happiness, and thus the creation of happiness should be what determines whether an action is moral or not. In other words, he claims that because something *is* the case, it *ought* to be the case. This is similar to arguing that since serial murderers enjoy killing people, then they *ought* to enjoy killing people. Or

[2]John Stuart Mill, *Utilitarianism*, Chapter IV, "Of What Sort of Proof the Principle of Utility Is Susceptible" (London: Parker, Son and Bourn, 1863).

even, since serial murderers do kill people, it is morally right to kill people. We cannot, of course, make that connection. In this same context, Mill argues that

> the only proof capable of being given that an object is visible is that people actually see it. The only proof that a sound is audible is that people hear it. . . In like manner, I apprehend, the sole evidence it is possible to produce that anything is desirable is that people do actually desire it.[3]

But Mill seems to be making a mistake here about the different meanings we attach to the words visible and desirable. By visible we just mean that people can see it, but by desirable we usually mean that people *should* desire it. Unless Mill makes the leap from "people do desire happiness" to "people should desire happiness," then his argument doesn't work. So Mill has committed the is/ought fallacy.

The Straw Man Fallacy   One of the hardest fallacies to detect is called the **straw man fallacy.** When an author commits the straw man fallacy, he changes the subject very subtly (from the "real man" to a "straw man" or irrelevant issue), so that he can attack it better. For example, if a person opposes prayer in the schools, she is often accused of being opposed to religion. This is a straw man because the issue is not religion as a whole, or even prayer in general, but only prayer in schools. An opposition to religion in general is easier to attack than the narrower issue of prayer in schools. Similarly, when the Equal Rights Amendment was being considered, one argument against it went like this:

> (P1) If the Equal Rights Amendment passes, then only unisex public toilets will be legal.

> (P2) Most people would be appalled to walk into a public toilet and find a person of the opposite sex in it.

> Therefore, (C) we should make sure the ERA doesn't pass.

This is a straw man argument. The point wasn't unisex toilets; the point was equal rights for women. Usually a person uses a straw man argument because he doesn't have very good reasons for opposing the original argument. So instead of knocking down the "real man" (the original argument), he erects a "straw man" and knocks it down instead, because a straw man is easier to topple.

PUTTING IT ALL TOGETHER

If the argument form is valid or strong, the premises are all true, and the author has not committed any fallacies, then (and only then) can you be reasonably sure that the author's conclusion is correct. Unfortunately,

---

[3]Mill, *Utilitarianism*, Chapter IV.

authors do not always make this easy for you. Reconstructing an argument is hard work. Evaluating premises can be even harder. However, before you can have any hope of deciding whether you agree or disagree with an author's conclusion (which we'll discuss in Chapter 6), you need to be able to analyze his argument. Let's put it all together.

Consider the following passage from Chapter V of Mill's *Utilitarianism:*

> In our survey of the various popular acceptations of justice, the term appeared generally to involve the idea of a personal right—a claim on the part of one or more individuals, like that which the law gives when it confers a proprietary or other legal right. Whether the injustice consists in depriving a person of a possession, or in breaking faith with him, or in treating him worse than he deserves, or worse than other people who have no greater claims—in each case the supposition implies two things: a wrong done, and some assignable person who is wronged. . . . It seems to me that this feature in the case—a right in some person, correlative to the moral obligation—constitutes the specific difference between justice and generosity or beneficence. Justice implies something which is not only right to do, and wrong not to do, but which some individual person can claim from us as his moral right. No one has a moral right to our generosity or beneficence because we are not morally bound to practice those virtues toward any given individual. . . .
>
> When we call anything a person's right, we mean that he has a valid claim on society to protect him in the possession of it, either by the force of law or by that of education and opinion. If he has what we consider a sufficient claim, on whatever account, to have something guaranteed to him by society, we say that he has a right to it. If we desire to prove that anything does not belong to him by right, we think this is done as soon as it is admitted that society ought not to take measure for securing it to him, but should leave him to chance or to his own exertions. Thus a person is said to have a right to what he can earn in fair professional competition, because society ought not to allow any other person to hinder him from endeavoring to earn in that manner as much as he can. But he has not a right to three hundred a year, though he may happen to be earning it; because society is not called on to provide that he shall earn that sum. . . .
>
> To have a right, then, is, I conceive, to have something which society ought to defend me in the possession of. If [an] objector goes on to ask why it ought, I can give him no other reason than general utility. If that expression does not seem to convey a sufficient feeling of the strength of the obligation, nor to account for the peculiar energy of the feeling, it is because there goes to the composition of the sentiment, not a rational only but also an animal element—the thirst for retaliation; and this thirst derives its intensity, as well as its moral justification, from the extraordinarily important and impressive kind of utility which is concerned. . . .

It appears from what has been said that justice is a name for certain moral requirements which, regarded collectively, stand higher in the scale of social utility, and are therefore of more paramount obligation, than any others, though particular cases may occur in which some other social duty is so important as to overrule any one of the general maxims of justice. Thus, to save a life, it may not only be allowable, but a duty, to steal or take by force the necessary food or medicine, or to kidnap and compel to officiate the only qualified medical practitioner. In such cases, as we do not call anything justice which is not a virtue, we usually say, not that justice must give way to some other moral principle, but that what is just in ordinary cases is, by reason of that other principle, not just in the particular case. . . .

Justice remains the appropriate name for certain social utilities which are vastly more important, and therefore more absolute and imperative, than any others are as a class (though not more so than others may be in particular cases); and which, therefore, ought to be, as well as naturally are, guarded by a sentiment, not only different in degree, but also in kind; distinguished from the milder feeling which attaches to the mere idea of promoting human pleasure or convenience at once by the more definite nature of its commands and by the sterner character of its sanctions.[4]

Now consider the following question:

What is Mill's argument regarding the connection between justice and utility?

Let's go through it following the five steps in analyzing an argument. First, the *conclusion* of this argument is that "Justice is simply the name for certain kinds of moral requirements which we consider most important on the scale of social utility." Second, the *premises* of the argument are as follows:

(P1) Justice implies something that it would be right to do and wrong not to do.

(P2) Justice involves a moral right on the part of an individual, which should be protected by society.

(P3) The reason society should protect this moral right is because we feel that what is involved is an "extraordinarily important and impressive kind" of happiness.

(P4) Protecting these moral rights creates a kind of happiness (utility) which we consider much more important than other kinds of happiness.

Third, *are there any words whose meanings need to be clarified?* Aside from his use of "social utility" and "the expedient" as synonyms for the general happiness, no. *Are there any hidden assumptions?* Only the principle of utility

[4]Mill, *Utilitarianism,* Chapter V, "Of the Connection Between Justice and Utility."

(that what makes actions right is that they lead to happiness), which isn't really hidden since this chapter follows his arguments defending that principle. *Are all his premises true?* That is debatable. In (P4) Mill claims that protecting our moral rights leads to a most important kind of happiness. Is that true? That is, are we really happier when people are treated fairly, when they are allowed to keep what they already own, and when like cases are treated alike? Sometimes, surely we are. But at least sometimes, it seems to me, we aren't. Of course, Mill responds to that by saying that in those cases, we don't want what is unjust, but some stronger principle overrides them, and thus that stronger principle is what is just. Fourth, *what is the structure of the argument?* It is probably meant to be deductive. That is, Mill seems to suggest that given the premises about what justice is and how we feel about it, it follows that "justice" is simply the name of certain actions that usually create more happiness than any of the alternatives. Fifth, does Mill *commit any fallacies or use any emotive language?* Probably not, unless you count the is/ought fallacy he commits in defending the original principle of utility. Is this a good argument? If you accept the principle of utility as a given, then this argument is probably a good one. Now you are ready to write your analysis. (I'll leave it to your imagination!)

6
WRITING FOR EVALUATION

The **evaluative essay** (or as it is sometimes called, the **argumentative essay**) is probably the most common essay required of philosophy students. In an evaluative essay, you are asked criticize or defend something you've read, usually an argument, theory, or essay. You are asked to make a judgment about whether the argument is a good or bad argument, whether the author is right or wrong, and whether you agree or disagree with him. However, if you just say that the author is right, that he has a good argument, and that you agree with him, all you have done is express your opinion. In an evaluative essay, your opinion must be supported by reliable evidence and strong reasoning. That is, you must provide an argument for why your interpretation of the author's argument or idea is the correct one.

Being critical of an argument does not mean being hostile to or intolerant of it. What it does mean is that you carefully consider the author's premises and conclusion and make a judgment about whether those premises are true, whether they provide relevant support for her conclusion, whether her examples and analogies are appropriate, whether she commits any fallacies, and so on. If you have not read Chapter 5, go back and do so now. You cannot write an evaluative essay without first being able to analyze the argument you are evaluating.

CHOOSING/DEVELOPING A THESIS

If your instructor allows you to choose your own topic (that is, what theory or essay you want to evaluate), think small. Trying to cover "What's wrong with Hume's theory of knowledge" in three to five pages is impossible. Of course, the longer the paper is supposed to be, the broader your thesis should be. At the introductory level, theses are generally broader than in more advanced classes. The less you know, the less you have to say about a

41

subject, and the more you know, the more you can say. It is, of course, possible to think *too* small. If you find that you have said everything you know in one page, you need to broaden your thesis. However, if the topic was assigned by your instructor, then the fact that you can only write one page is an indication that you aren't thinking deeply or thoroughly enough.

As we saw in Chapter 5, there are two general ways to criticize an argument. The first is to *assess the structure of the argument*—is it valid or invalid, strong or weak? Do the premises provide relevant and sufficient evidence for thinking the conclusion is true? In fact, many arguments that you read in the history of philosophy probably will not be deductively invalid or inductively weak. Thus, the second way to criticize an argument is to *criticize the content of the argument*. Are the premises true? Does the author equivocate about the meaning of his terms? Does he commit any informal fallacies? Once you have answered these questions to your own satisfaction, you need to formulate your thesis—your opinion regarding what is wrong (or right) with the argument.

THE EVALUATIVE ESSAY

The evaluative essay usually follows a particular pattern. The beginning of the essay, the introduction, should include not only a full statement of whether you agree or disagree with the author, but also a preliminary statement of your reasons for why you agree or disagree. Of course, until you analyze the argument, you won't know whether (and why) you agree or disagree. Thus, writing your introduction will be one of the last things you do.

In the body of the essay, you will need to state the author's argument precisely, completely, and in a detailed way. You need to analyze the argument, as we did in Chapter 5, by carefully identifying both the premises and the structure of the argument. Then you should critically evaluate the argument. In doing so, you need to make it clear what you object to, give your reasons for why you object, show that you have thought about how the author might respond to your objection, and consider how seriously your objection damages the argument.

Finally, in your conclusion, you should provide a brief summary and review of your argument, and perhaps give an indication of any further implications it might have. Typically, your conclusion will be fairly brief and should not be too repetitive.

EXAMPLE: WILLIAM PALEY'S ARGUMENT FOR THE EXISTENCE OF GOD

Say you have been assigned or have chosen to argue against William Paley's design argument, in which he claims to prove God's existence. First, consider the following passage from Paley:

In crossing the heath, suppose I pitched my foot against a *stone*, and were asked how the stone came to be there, I might possibly answer, that, for anything I knew to the contrary, it had lain there forever; nor would it, perhaps, be very easy to show the absurdity of this answer. But suppose I found a *watch* upon the ground, and it should be inquired how the watch happened to be in that place, I should hardly think of the answer which I had before given—that for anything I knew, the watch might have always been there. Yet why should not this answer serve for the watch as well as for the stone? Why is it not as admissible in the second case as in the first? For this reason, and for no other, viz., that, when we come to inspect the watch, we perceive . . . that its several parts are framed and put together for a purpose, for example, that they are so formed and adjusted as to produce motion, and that motion so regulated as to point out the hour of the day; that, if the different parts had been differently shaped from what they are, if a different size from what they are, or placed after any other manner, or in any other order than that in which they are placed, either no motion would have been carried on in the machine, or none which would have answered the use that is now served by it. . . . This mechanism being observed . . . the inference, we think, is inevitable, that the watch must have had a maker; that there must have existed, at some place or other, an artificer or artificers [creators] who formed it for the purpose which we find it actually to answer; who comprehended its construction, and designed its use.

I. Nor would it, I apprehend, weaken the conclusion that we had never seen a watch made; that we had never known an artist capable of making one; that we were altogether incapable of executing such a workmanship ourselves, or of understanding in what manner it was performed. . . . Ignorance of this kind exalts our opinion of the unseen and unknown artist's skill, if he be unseen and unknown, but raises no doubt in our minds of the existence and agency of such an artist, at some former time, and in some place or other. . . .

II. Neither, secondly, would it invalidate our conclusion, that the watch sometimes went wrong, or that it seldom went exactly right. . . . It is not necessary that a machine be perfect in order to show with what design it was made. . . .

III. Nor, thirdly, would it bring any uncertainty into the argument if there were a few parts of the watch concerning which we could not discover, or had not yet discovered, in what manner they conduced to the general effect; or even some parts concerning which we could not ascertain whether they conducted to that effect in any manner whatever. . . .

VII. And [a person would be] not less surprised to be informed, that the watch in his hand was nothing more than the result of the laws of *metallic* nature. It is a perversion of language to assign any law as the efficient, operative cause of anything. A law presupposes as an agent, for it is only the mode according to which an agent proceeds; it implies a power; for it is the order according to which that power acts. Without this agent, without this power, which are both distinct from itself the *law* does nothing, is nothing. . . .

Every indication of contrivance, every manifestation of design, which existed in the watch, exists in the works of nature; with the difference, on the side of nature, of being greater and more, and that in a degree which exceeds all computation. . . .[1]

Summarize Paley's Argument

An ideal way to start your evaluative essay on Paley's design argument would be to write a brief summary (see Chapter 3) of his argument. Notice that in the summary below, I also provide examples and specifics to make the various points clear.

> According to Paley, if I found a watch while I was out walking, I wouldn't think that it, like a stone, had just been there forever. Because the watch is very complex and clearly has a purpose (telling time), it is obvious that it had a designer, a creator, someone who made it. Even if I had never seen a watch made, or known a watchmaker, or could make a watch myself, I would still know that someone made it. Also, just because the watch is broken doesn't mean no one designed it. The fact that it doesn't fulfill its intended purpose means that it *has* an intended purpose. If there are parts of the watch that I don't understand, or that don't seem to do anything (like a person's appendix?), that just makes me respect the designer more. If someone told me that the watch was the way it was because of the coming together of the "laws of metallic nature" I'd think they were nuts. Thus, it seems clear that the watch must have had a designer, who designed it to tell time, and a creator, who put all the pieces together so that they do tell time. Now, Paley says, consider the universe. Everything about the complexity and the purpose of the watch is even more true about the universe. By analogy then, if the watch must have had a designer/creator, then so must the universe.

Analyze the Argument

The next thing you need to do is analyze that argument, as you learned to do in Chapter 5. First, outline Paley's premises and conclusions:

Part One:

(P1): A watch is a complex object which contains wheels and glass and hands, all of which have been put together so that they work together to tell time.

[1]William Paley, *Natural Theology* (London: Longmans, Green & Co., 1838), pp. 211–16.

(P2): This is not the kind of thing that could happen by chance or by accident.

(C): Thus, we think the watch must have had a designer/maker.

Part Two:

(P1): But look at how complex the universe is—or even any small part of the universe.

(P2): By analogy, if a watch must have had a maker, then something even more complex (like the universe) must also have had a maker.

(C): Thus, the universe must have had a maker—God.

This is the main structure of Paley's argument. I left out some of his points (numbered I–VII in his essay) because they are actually replies to objections rather than premises in the main argument. Notice that Paley's argument takes the form of what is called an "argument from analogy." He is saying: Object A (the watch) has qualities x, y, and z. Object B (the universe) also has qualities x, y, and z. Since object B is very like object A, and since object A has quality w (having a designer), then object B probably does too. This is the general form of any analogy. The claim is that since the two objects are similar in a number of ways, they are probably also similar in the one important way. Notice that an argument from analogy is an *inductive argument*. That is, it only proves that object B *probably* also has quality w.

Describe Your Position

The next step is to write a description of your own position, summarizing your own argument briefly. For example:

> I intend to argue that Paley's argument does not work, because although it provides an explanation for where the universe came from, it is ultimately unsatisfactory for a number of reasons.

Once you have analyzed the argument, you will have discovered any weak points—false or doubtful premises, informal fallacies, premises that don't support the conclusion, and so on. Now is the time to do some hard thinking about how successful you find the argument. Does it work? Are there problems? Has the author claimed to prove more than he has proved? What do you agree or disagree with and why? Must his conclusion be rejected completely or can his premises provide support for a different, perhaps more restricted, conclusion?

There are several things to keep in mind as you prepare your evaluation. A bad argument for a conclusion does not prove that the conclusion is false. All it proves is that it's a bad argument—that is, that *these* premises do not provide good evidence for the conclusion. So be sure you don't conclude that since Paley's argument doesn't work, that proves that God doesn't exist.

Keep in mind also that your instructor is not as interested in *what* you think about Paley's argument, but in the reasons and arguments that you provide for *why* you think it. Now flesh out your earlier statement of your position:

> I think Paley is wrong that his design argument proves that God exists. In the first place, a watch isn't very much like the universe. There are no laws of "metallic nature" that could explain it. However, there are laws of physics, chemistry, and evolution that can explain how the universe came to be the way it is. My second objection is that many objects (like watches) have more than one maker or designer—doesn't this imply that there might be more than one God? Also, once the designer or creator makes a watch, he goes on to something else, and doesn't pay attention to it any more. So God might not care about us, or might not still be involved with us (by causing miracles, etc.). In addition, a watchmaker is not all-powerful or all-knowing, so that may show that God isn't either. Finally, even if God (or gods) explain why the universe is the way it is, it still leaves us with something unexplained—who designed/created God? God must have had a creator (call him God2). But then God2 must have had a creator also—God3, etc. Does this actually solve anything?

Outline Your Essay

Now, put everything together into an outline. An outline provides structure for your essay, helping you to organize your thoughts and to spot any weak points in your argument. It also insures that you don't get side-tracked from the main issue. The outline can help you recognize problems with the structure of your argument, as well as any possible weak points. When you begin with an outline, you establish control over your essay. Of course, it is entirely possible that as you write you will begin to deviate from the original outline. This is perfectly natural and sometimes useful. I began each chapter of this book with a *very* rough outline, but very few chapters ended up exactly following the outline. Your outline isn't written in stone. It is not supposed to restrict and confine you in any way. It is simply a tool to make your writing easier and to improve the final product. It insures that when you begin writing, you already have a clear idea of where you want to go. Here is a sample outline for an argument written in response to the Paley essay:

I. Introduction:
  A. Paley's argument from design is inadequate to prove the existence of God.
  B. While it may explain where the universe came from, it is ultimately unsatisfactory for a number of reasons.
II. Paley's argument:
  A. Part one:
    1. A watch is a complex object which contains wheels and glass and hands, all of which have been put together so that they work together to tell time.

     2. This is not the kind of thing that could happen by chance or by accident.

     3. Thus, we think the watch must have had a designer/maker.

  B. Part two:

     1. But look at how complex the universe is—or even any small part of the universe.

     2. By analogy, if a watch must have had a maker, then something even more complex (like the universe) must also have had a maker.

     3. Thus, the universe must have had a maker—God.

  C. Paley's best responses to objections:

     1. Never seen a watch made or known a watchmaker or know how to make a watch ourselves.

     2. Watch sometimes doesn't work right.

     3. Some parts of the watch that I don't understand how or whether they help it keep time.

     4. The laws of metallic nature just came together in such a way to produce the watch.

III. Critique of Paley's argument:

  A. Paley's design argument relies on an analogy between a watch and the universe (or some specific part of the universe). This is not a good analogy because while a watch cannot be explained by "laws of metallic nature," the universe can be explained by laws of physics, chemistry, evolution, etc.

  B. Even if his analogy worked, it still wouldn't prove what he claims it does.

     1. If Paley's argument works, all it shows is that someone created the world—it doesn't show that the creator is God: all-knowing, all-powerful, etc.

     2. Many (most) complex things have one or more people who have designed them (like the architects who design a house) as well as one or more people who have created them (like the carpenters, etc., who build the house). The more complex something is, the more likely it is that it has had more than one designer/creator. This implies that there are probably many designers/creators of the universe.

     3. Even if Paley's argument works, it doesn't explain where God came from. If the universe is complex and has a purpose, then God must be at least as complex as the universe (or probably more—think how much more complex the watchmaker is than the watch), so someone must have designed/created him, too.

IV. How Paley might reply:

The only response that I can see that Paley can make is to weaken his argument so that he only claims to prove that someone (or ones) designed/created the universe; that he or they may not be all-powerful, all-knowing, loving, etc.; that maybe he or they created the laws of physics, etc.; and that he or they are somehow "self-creating" (but that would require an argument to prove and he doesn't offer one).

V. Conclusion

Paley's argument can *at most* show that something designed/created the universe, but it not only can't show that that "something" is *one* God, who is all-powerful and all-knowing and who cares about us and causes miracles, but it also doesn't really solve the problem of creation—it only pushes it back one more level. If Paley's argument works, then we no longer have to ask where the universe came from and why it is the way it is, but we do have to ask where God (or gods) came from and why he (they) is the way that he (they) is. Since this is obviously *not* what Paley thinks he proves, his argument is ultimately unsatisfying and unsound.

Notice that I wrote this outline with complete sentences (mostly) and I made it as comprehensive as possible. The outline runs to several pages all by itself. Writing an essay from it should prove relatively easy. I've already made most of my points in the outline. To write the essay, all I have to do is put these ideas into coherent sentences and paragraphs with the appropriate connecting words and thoughts. In fact, most of the hard work has been done by the time I finish the outline.

Write the Essay

Just because I wrote a very complete and comprehensive outline doesn't mean that I won't change my mind as I begin to write the paper. I have to flesh out my ideas and objections to the argument, and as I do so, I may realize that some of my points aren't as strong as I thought, that I have misinterpreted something Paley said or that there is a more sympathetic way to interpret what he said, or that there are other, better objections to his argument than the ones I initially came up with. Your outline is not sacred— change it at will. Just be sure that you wind up with an organized essay. If you change your outline, then when you finish writing your essay, re-outline it to be sure that the structure is still clear. If the essay wanders off on tangents, re-outlining will help you recognize the problems.

CONCLUDING REMARKS

Don't forget the principle of charity mentioned in Chapter 2. The author found his argument particularly compelling—or else he wouldn't have written it. Put yourself into his shoes and try to figure out why a rational, well-meaning person would accept the premises and conclusion. Your evaluation should be appropriate and fair, your tone should be respectful throughout the essay, and you should avoid committing fallacies or using emotive language. Despite the fact that you disagree with the author's conclusion and/or his argument, you should not be intolerant, abusive, or malicious in your criticism.

Evaluating someone else's argument is good practice before you try to create your own arguments, which we will discuss in the next chapter. In discovering and criticizing common mistakes, you can give yourself a jump start on avoiding them in your own writing. It is much easier to criticize someone else's argument than it is to come up with a new and original argument of your own. As you may already have discovered in your philosophical reading, much of the history of philosophy consists of one philosopher discussing and evaluating the arguments of an earlier philosopher. Any philosophical idea, argument, or theory is fair game. A theory worth holding is a theory worth criticizing. If it can't stand up to critical evaluation, then it isn't worth believing in the first place.

SAMPLE ESSAY

This essay was written by a junior mathematics major in an upper-division course on "Ethics and Feminism." It is not perfect, of course. Notice for example, the extensive use of quotations. While this use *may* be excessive, the student may have quoted the original essay so thoroughly in order to prove that the author of the essay really said what she is accusing him of saying. This essay might also have been improved by an introductory paragraph explaining what the student intended to say about the essay she is criticizing. Her thesis statement is never fully articulated until the last line of her essay. However, she does a reasonably good job of analyzing and evaluating the original essay and there is some subtle use of irony.

Sex and Sports

In his essay "Sex and Sports,"[2] George Gilder states that athletics for men "is an ideal of purity and truth" (231) and that the presence of women destroys the illusion of the ideal. According to Gilder, sports "embody for men a moral universe" (230). Team sports teach men to cooperate and to learn the importance of loyalty, self-sacrifice, and toughness in "pursuing a noble ideal" (230). Male competitions are "gravely compromised" (232) by participation by women, for women reduce the game from a "religious male rite" (232) to mere physical exercise. He goes on to say that sports are perhaps the single most important rite in male socialization.

Gilder "supports" his argument by claiming that no matter how hard a woman athlete trains, or how good she might be, she will never be more than a "somewhat distorted and inferior reflection" (231) of her male counterpart. A woman succeeds in "male" sports despite her physique, but her

[2]George Gilder, "Sex and Sports," in *Sexual Suicide* (New York: Bantam, 1973).

performance is "flawed" because it is not a "natural and beautiful fulfill-ment" of her body (231). Female participation in sports is, according to Gilder, an exhibition of "physical repression and distortion" (231). This "feminist threat" weakens and destroys the "ritual nature . . . moral purpose . . . [and] symbolic aspirations" (232) of sports, especially for boys.

Gilder's largest worry seems to be that female participation in sports somehow destroys the lessons of "group morality" that boys learn from them. Gilder obviously does not believe in what one could call the "basic equality" of the sexes. What is important for the social growth of a boy should, in turn, be important for the social growth of a girl. Gilder says that boys need to learn cooperation, the importance of loyalty and self-sacrifice, and the "indispensable sensation of competition in solidarity" (230). How-ever, apparently it is not important that girls learn these things too.

Paradoxically, what seems rather evident from his essay, is that Gilder's real complaint lies in the fact that he feels girls somehow subvert the mas-culinity of boys when playing games with them. He states that a certain female Olympic runner can run "almost as fast as a male adolescent" (231), yet when junior high girls play against their male peers it is "disastrous" for some of the boys—those same adolescents to whom he compared Bragina, the "Olympic Marvel" (231). However, it is not only young boys who risk the chance of being out-done by a woman. Gilder feels that when men compete with women, they always keep something in reserve so that they can "rationalize" their defeat. If a man is necessarily superior to a woman in sports (which is what Gilder would have one believe) there should be no reason for rationalization of defeat—because there should be no defeat.

Gilder advocates a "separate but equal" status for female athletes. As long as she retains the grace, agility, and beauty of her body—that "perfec-tion of sensuous form and movement" (235)—then that sport is an accept-able one. Gilder's claim is that women should and can never compete on an equal basis with men. A woman can bring grace and style to "recreational sports," and even, perhaps, be "better" than her male counterpart, aesthet-ically. But this should take place only outside of "serious competition" where the activities seem "unfeminine" when carried to the "extremes of international competition" (235). Gilder seems to want to exclude women from public attention for no better reason than that he feels such promi-nence in athletics is "unfeminine" and not aesthetically pleasing. He appears to drop his argument about "group morality," which clearly would not apply in this case, and has decided to appeal to women's vanity. One wouldn't want to be pointed out as a distortion or a deformation—surely every woman has more pride than that.

These premises are questionable at best; when one reads more closely, it seems clear that Gilder wants to exclude women from male-dominated sports just because they are women, and perhaps because they might surpass male achievement. When women distort sports thus, he claims that there is some "treacherous danger of psychic damage" (232). Apparently those deli-cate male psyches are not a hindrance to their superior performances—that is, as long as there are no women present. For women "destroy the illusion of the ideal" (232)—the ideal that men are naturally physically superior, and, if one listens to Gilder, somehow morally superior. He seems to feel, however, that men won't achieve that moral superiority if, at age 15, they are forced to play baseball with their female peers.

One would have to question that statement. There are, presumably, two explanations—neither of which is acceptable to all. Either women already possess that superior morality and thus it is unnecessary for them to learn it through sports, or else women don't need to learn that morality; for whatever reason, it is not important that women learn cooperation, loyalty, etc. Gilder would certainly disagree with the former, and many would disagree with the latter. If this socialization is so important for young boys—assuming that boys are at least morally equal and not inferior to girls—then it follows that perhaps this "male socialization" should be extended to women.

Even if one accepts his conclusion that the presence of girls in sports during the formative years is detrimental to the boys, one would still have to question his statement that women should not be in "serious competition." Or could it be that if an adult woman is competing against one of her contemporaries, she will still damage his fragile male psyche? If his all-male athletic experience in his youth had nurtured his psychic well-being as Gilder claims, then the presence of a woman in competition with him at that late date would be nothing more than an irritant. Gilder says that if we allow this old form of male socialization to continue, boys will develop to their fullest potential, which naturally makes them athletically superior to girls. Yet, once again, Gilder has contradicted himself. It brings one back to the tennis player who kept a little in reserve so that he could rationalize his defeat by his girlfriend. This inconsistency in Gilder's argument occurs again and again so that one wonders how Gilder rationalizes these discrepancies.

To accept Gilder's conclusion—which is essentially that women should stay out of male-dominated sports—one would have to accept his premises, which seem shaky at best. Women are not the physical equals of men and thus cannot play games as well, and therefore shouldn't play at all; yet, at the same time, women shouldn't play games because there is a reasonably good chance that they will win and thus damage fragile male egos. One wonders how Gilder reconciles this fragile, easily damaged psyche with the natural superiority, both physical and moral, that he attributes to men. The inconsistencies in his argument force one to conclude that, although some of his premises may in fact be correct, but not proven, his premises do not support his conclusion, and thus his argument is invalid, and can, essentially, be disregarded.

7
WRITING FOR SYNTHESIS

A **synthesis essay** is primarily a *thesis defense paper:* That is, you take a position on an issue and then defend it. It involves bringing together elements of several different arguments to create a new whole. You will rarely be asked to write a synthesis essay on an in-class exam—usually it will be assigned as a longer, out-of-class essay. However, a synthesis essay is not a research paper that merely reports what other people have said. Nor is it simply an expression of your feelings or emotions. It is not simply a collection of stories or examples. And it is not a compilation of quotations from a number of different sources. A synthesis essay is, at its most basic, an attempt to persuade someone of something. As with evaluative essays, you must give reasons and present evidence for why your position is correct, and then you must defend your thesis against objections. You argue that there are much better reasons for accepting your thesis than there are for rejecting it, or much better reasons for accepting it than for accepting any of the alternatives.

Unlike the evaluative essay, however, your position will not represent an evaluation of someone else's theory; it will be an original position that you yourself believe and want to support. I use the term "original" loosely, of course. You may argue that God doesn't exist, that abortion is not immoral, or that life has no meaning, and, of course, plenty of people will have argued for these same conclusions before you. What will be original, with luck, will be—not your conclusion—but your argument proving that conclusion. Of course, in philosophy you can rarely hope to prove that your thesis is absolutely, positively true, but you should try to show why an ordinary, rational person should believe it. Unless you are extraordinarily innovative, you probably won't come up with a position that is completely original. Don't worry—your instructor doesn't expect it!

We all have presented our own arguments in favor of something at some time. When you try to convince your friends to go see the movie you want to see instead of an alternative, you present them with reasons and evidence for why your chosen movie is the better choice. When you try to convince your parents that you need a new car, or a guitar, or a tattoo, you use an argument to convince them. (And I don't, of course, mean an argument in the sense that you get angry and scream and yell. Once you do that, you have given up on the kind of argument I'm talking about.) An argumentative essay in philosophy requires more care and depth than these kinds of arguments. The kind of evidence that may be persuasive in casual conversation is usually not acceptable in a philosophy class.

What is important in a thesis defense paper is not usually *what* position you argue for, but *how* you argue for it. Recall this example from Chapter 1:

> Do universals like Truth and Beauty really exist? Provide an argument to support your answer.

Your instructor probably isn't concerned with whether you think that universals exist or don't exist, but you must decide which position you think is true, so that you can build your essay around that claim. This kind of essay may well be the most difficult one you ever write. Because of that, it is important that you choose your thesis well. *Choose a thesis that is worth arguing for.* Only when a conclusion is not obvious is it necessary to argue for it. If you choose a position so obvious that practically no one disagrees, or if you choose a controversial position on a trivial subject, you are wasting your time. If your instructor provides you with a choice (as in the example above), then you need only choose to argue one side or the other. It is, of course, much easier to argue for something you believe. On the other hand, be open to the possibility that as you write and accumulate evidence, you may decide to change your mind.

OUTLINE

It is very important that you create at least a rough outline before you begin writing. (See Chapter 6.) The structure of a synthesis essay is very simple:

I. Introduction: State your thesis (conclusion).
II. Give your reasons and supporting evidence (premises) for that conclusion.
III. Show not only that your premises are true, but that they prove the conclusion.
IV. Present objections to your position (counter-arguments).
V. Explain why each of those objections fail.
VI. Conclusion: Summarize and review what you have accomplished and what it means.

This is the most basic of outlines. Any synthesis essay you write will take this form or something very like it. The trick is to begin with this bare outline, and then add to it.

Suppose you want to argue that it is not morally permissible to use non-human animals to test products intended for human use. Part I of your outline would read:

I. Introduction:
It is not morally permissible to use nonhuman animals to test products intended for human use.

In this first part of your essay you will briefly state how you plan to prove your thesis. You also may want to explain what the issue is and why you think it is important. You can put all of this in your outline if you want to. The more complete your outline is, the easier your essay will be to write.

Part II, then, should be your reasons for why you think your thesis is true. Refer back to the way we analyzed arguments in Chapter 5. You need to use these same steps in creating your own argument. Lay out each premise and the conclusion:

II. Argument:
A. Since animals feel pain, they should not be subjected to any unnecessary suffering.
B. If an experiment does not benefit the animal, then any suffering is unnecessary.
C. Experiments or tests for products intended for human use do not benefit the animal.
D. Thus, animals should not be used to test products intended for human use.

In Part III you will show why your premises should be accepted. In fact, you may need to provide an argument for one or more of your premises in order to show why it is true. Part III is not so easy to outline. To help you in your writing, you should probably at least indicate some of your reasons for thinking your premises are true. For example:

III. Truth of premises:
A. If utilitarianism is true, then the only relevant moral criteria are pleasure and pain. Animals clearly feel pleasure and pain just as humans do.
B. Define unnecessary suffering, and show why tests that don't benefit the animal are unnecessary.

Notice a couple of things in this outline. First, I have used complete sentences. This isn't strictly necessary, but it is a good habit to get into, since writing the essay will be much easier if you are starting with complete sentences. Second, in Part III, I reveal a particular bias I am taking in this essay—that is, I am assuming that utilitarianism is true. If it is not, then my argument will not work. Of course, I could add another argument to Part II (call it IIa) that will insure that my conclusion is accepted, even by those who are not utilitarians.

IIa. Argument IIa:
   A. A creature has rights just in case there are things it has an interest in that society should protect.
   B. While animals do not have the same interests as we do (for example, they aren't concerned about making money or getting a good job), they do have other interests like ours (like staying alive and having enough food to eat and being free from pain).
   C. If society has a duty to protect the interests of human beings not to be harmed unnecessarily (because people have an interest in not being harmed), then society also has a duty to protect the interests of nonhuman beings that also have an interest in not being harmed.
   D. Thus, animals cannot be used to test products that will cause harm to them, especially if they will not receive any benefit from those products.

Part IIIa will then provide your reasons for thinking the premises of this argument are true. Some of the premises may require arguments to prove them, others won't.

IIIa. Truth of premises in argument IIa:
   A. Say why having interests implies having rights that society should protect.
   B. Say why animals' interests are qualitatively similar to human interests.

In Part IV you will respond to objections to your position. This may involve responding to things some other philosopher has actually said, or it may involve responding to possible objections. For example, many people object to utilitarianism. You probably can't respond to this objection (since doing so would involve defending utilitarianism, which is a whole different paper). However, you can point out that your second argument does not depend on utilitarianism. Another possible objection is that there is something unique about human beings that gives them rights, and it is not, probably, merely the fact that they have interests. That is, some people would say that although animals do have an interest in not being harmed, simply having that interest does not imply that society should protect that interest.

Alternatively or additionally, you may want to consider particular arguments advanced by philosophers regarding why animals do not have the kinds of rights you claim they do. For example, Carl Cohen argues that animals are not the kind of beings that can have rights, since having a moral right implies being able to understand right from wrong, and animals are not capable of this. Therefore, anything we can use animals for to help humans is justified.[1] So Part IV of your outline may look like this:

[1]Carl Cohen, "The Case for the Use of Animals in Biomedical Research," *The New England Journal of Medicine* 315, no. 14 (October 1, 1986), pp. 865–70.

IV. Objections:
  A. Animal pain, unlike human pain, is not morally relevant.
  B. Some suffering may be necessary, even if it doesn't benefit the one who suffers.
  C. Animals don't have the same rights as humans.
  D. Cohen's argument about why animals don't have rights.

In Part V you need to respond to those objections and explain why they fail to refute your argument. So, for example:

V. Response to objections:
  A. Pain is pain—animal pain isn't qualitatively different from human pain.
  B. Fairness and justice require that any suffering inflicted must be either deserved or for the sufferer's own good.
  C. The arguments for why animals don't have the same rights as humans are unconvincing.
  D. Cohen is wrong about what it means to have rights.

Note that while I have put all the objections in Part IV and all the responses in Part V, it would probably be better to write the essay this way:

IV. Objections and responses:
  A. Objection: Animal pain isn't morally relevant; human pain is. Response: Pain is pain—animal pain isn't qualitatively different from human pain, and so on.

Finally, Part VI is the conclusion of your essay (which, as we know, restates the conclusion of your argument). In addition, Part VI should indicate some of the consequences of accepting that conclusion. So,

VI. Conclusion:
  A. Nonhuman animals should not be used to test products for human use.
  B. This means that:
    1. We should not use animals to test cosmetics, household products, medical procedures, or medicines.
    2. The development of new medical technology and new medicines will probably slow down.
    3. If we used people as test subjects, we could speed up the development of new procedures and medicines, but we cannot.
    4. My argument(s) shows that we shouldn't use animals for these purposes either, even though not using them may have some bad consequences.

Your Part VI may not be this detailed, but when I prepare an outline, I try to include all the important points I want to make so that I don't forget them!

If you begin with a very complete outline like this one, you will find writing your essay much easier. Even if you decide not to write an outline before you begin, you should certainly try to outline the essay after you finish writing it. (If you do start with an outline and you depart from it, you should probably outline again after you finish.) If, when your essay is completed, you can write a fairly coherent and intelligible outline, then you know that the essay itself is fairly coherent and intelligible. If, on the other hand, you cannot create a plausible outline, then you know that the essay has problems that must be fixed. Organizational and structural problems will be very clear in the outline. Of course, there may be other problems with the essay that the outline won't catch, but since coherence, clarity, and consistency are some of the most important elements in a philosophical essay, take my advice and write an outline!

EVIDENCE

Notice that my outline shows that I have reasons for why I believe my thesis is true. I do not simply say "I feel" or "I believe." Readers don't care how you *feel* about animal testing. Their feelings may not be the same as yours. In order to persuade them that your feelings are right, you have to provide an argument that consists of reasons why any rational, well-meaning person should also feel as you do. Don't mistake having an opinion for being right. A thesis that is not supported by reasons or evidence is not an argument. Your instructor is less interested in what you believe (your thesis) than she is in how well you argue for that thesis. When you do not provide reasons in support of your thesis, or when you provide weak or poorly supported reasons, you weaken your essay.

Use the strongest and most convincing reasons (premises) you can find to support your position. As I suggested, you may need to provide subarguments to show why your premises are true. Many of your premises will not need such support, but at least some of them probably will. Not only must your reasons be convincing, but you must be sure that together they form a chain of reasoning that will allow your reader to arrive at the same conclusion you do. This means that your conclusion probably should not contradict common sense. If your conclusion is too far out in left field, you will lose your reader fairly quickly. At the same time, simply because your conclusion seems to contradict common sense is not necessarily a reason for not defending it. *If* you make your thesis as clear as possible, and *if* you make sure that every point in your essay supports that thesis, and *if* each of those supporting points is clear in itself, and *if* you can make it clear how the structure of the argument works—that is, how the premises fit together to establish the truth of the conclusion—then any possible thesis is fair game. Of course, all those *ifs* apply even if your thesis doesn't contradict common sense.

In providing evidence for your conclusion, do not rely solely on examples. An example usually is not enough to establish the truth of a point. But using examples *can* help to clarify points, illustrate the point being made, or suggest what is wrong with a counter-argument. Good examples can improve an essay dramatically, while bad or irrelevant examples really detract from the quality of an essay. Use examples wisely, but use them (see Chapter 4).

Notice that the kind of evidence offered in support of the thesis about animal testing was not scientific or religious in nature. Philosophical questions can almost never be solved by appeals to science, experience, personal feelings, psychology, or social causes. They cannot be resolved by appeals to authorities ("Kant said so" or "The Bible says so"). A philosophical question can only be answered by the process of providing reasonable and relatively unambiguous reasons that fit together in an appropriate way so that they either establish the truth of the conclusion or at least make it more likely to be true than not.

You should also be careful not to claim to have proved more than you actually have. If you can only show that something is true in *most* cases, then don't claim that it is *always* true. For example, in using a utilitarian argument to oppose animal testing, you need to make it clear that in at least some cases, utilitarianism suggests that animal testing is acceptable—that is, when the pain caused to the animal is far outweighed by the amount of happiness or pleasure gained by humans.

Remember the distinction made in Chapter 5 between deductive and inductive arguments? Often it is impossible to achieve the deductive standard of proving your thesis with certainty. If so, acknowledge the uncertainty and settle for less. If you can't prove beyond any doubt that animal testing is wrong, don't claim that you can. However, if you can show that there is a strong probability that animal testing is wrong, or that in most cases animal testing is wrong, or even that the evidence opposing animal testing seems to be stronger than the evidence in favor of it, then say so, and realize that this is quite an accomplishment in itself.

Students often think that philosophy simply consists of differences in opinion. It's just my opinion against your opinion, and because everyone's opinion is as good as anyone else's, there is no way to decide who is right. Many people think that anyone who believes something strongly enough and expresses himself loudly enough deserves to have his "argument" respected. This is not true in philosophy or in any other academic area. I tell my students that philosophy doesn't traffic in opinions, it traffics in arguments. That is, while people do have different opinions, the way to decide who is right is to decide who presents the best argument—in the form of evidence, reasons, and proofs. Shouting your opinion isn't any better than whispering it. And simply because many people agree with your opinion is not grounds for thinking your opinion is right. Opinions must be supported by reasons. If they are not, then they *are* merely opinions, and they probably *are* equal. The moral of this story is that without reasons to support your thesis, your "argument" is relatively useless.

COUNTER-ARGUMENTS

In the basic outline, Parts IV and V involved presenting counter-arguments (or objections to your argument) and showing why the counter-arguments fail. Notice that in my outline for the essay on animal testing, I responded to three kinds of objections. One objection (Cohen's) had to do with a direct objection to my thesis, but not to the particular argument I presented in support of that thesis. Several of the other counter-arguments were objections to particular premises within my argument. Also notice that one objection (Cohen's again) was an argument that someone actually used (and thus should be footnoted—see Chapter 8). The other objections were just sort of generic objections that someone *could* use against my argument.

Your argument will be much stronger if you consider objections and counter-arguments. By showing that you are aware of the concerns of others, and by showing that your own argument can withstand their criticisms, you strengthen your position considerably. On the other hand, if you find you cannot adequately respond to their criticisms, then there is something wrong with your argument. However, don't fall into the trap of using weak counter-arguments that are certain to be unconvincing. Weak counter-arguments simply make your own argument weaker. If you find that you can't refute the counter-arguments, then you may need to consider changing your own thesis. You may decide to change sides completely (for example, argue that animal testing *is* morally justified), or you may decide simply to weaken your thesis (and argue that animal testing *probably* or *usually* isn't justified). Controversial issues are controversial simply because there are good, persuasive arguments on both sides, which well-meaning people of good faith accept.

While I presented four possible counter-arguments in my outline, unless you are writing a fairly lengthy essay, you probably will not need so many. (Also, in a shorter essay, you can probably only present one of the two arguments, either the utilitarian one or the rights one.) Often you will choose your thesis on the basis of some essay with which you disagree. If so, use that essay as a counter-argument. In any case, it is very important that you keep your mind open enough about your thesis that you can understand and reconstruct the arguments of those who disagree with you. This means that you must try to fairly and accurately represent those positions with which you disagree. I could tell you that this practice is good for you and it builds character, but I'm not your mother. What I can tell you is that presenting and refuting counter-arguments contributes to a *much* better (translation: higher grade) essay than not doing so.

PUTTING IT ALL TOGETHER

The Introduction

When you begin to write your essay based on your outline, don't start with the introduction. I know that is counter-intuitive, but you should probably write your introduction last—or at least expect to come back to it after you have finished the rest of the essay and done some major revisions. The reason for writing the introduction last is that, even with a good outline, you will rarely be sure of exactly what you are going to argue and how you are going to argue for it. Your introduction needs not only to state your thesis, but also to summarize how you intend to prove that thesis, and you may not be able to describe that in any detail when you start out. Begin by writing the body of the paper. Start with your argument and its premises and the connections and inter-relationships between them.

When you do write your introduction, your thesis statement probably won't be the first sentence. You need to build up to it. What is the issue at hand? Why is it important? What is the context in which this issue is located? Don't start with a dictionary definition: "Webster's defines *euthanasia* as . . . ." Don't start with a huge generalization: "Throughout history, philosophers have been concerned about . . . ." Don't start with: "In this paper I will . . . ." Don't begin your essay with your first premise—at this early stage, your reader has no idea why it's relevant. Do begin by establishing your topic and discussing its importance, relevance, and perhaps timeliness. For example, in the essay on animal testing, you could begin by stating that animals are used for testing a variety of products for human use. You might then go on to give some examples of the kind of testing that is done, highlighting the pain and suffering caused to the animal (since one of your main points is going to be that the animals suffer).

By the end of your first, or maybe second, paragraph you should have stated your thesis, so that the reader has no doubt what position you plan to defend. By the end of your introduction, the reader should also have a reasonably clear idea about how you plan to prove that thesis. Your introduction should be so clear that even someone who knows nothing of ethics or animal testing (for example) can understand not only what the issue is, but also what your position on it is, and, in a general way, how you plan to go about persuading him that you are right.

Here is an example of a brief introduction for the essay on animal testing. Notice that if the essay were to be a very long one, the introduction would probably need to be longer as well.

> When manufacturers of household cleaners, women's cosmetics, or prescription drugs develop a new product, the Food and Drug Administration requires that they test those products on animals in order to show that they are safe for human use. One common test that is used is called the Draize test. In the Draize test, rabbits' eyes are sewed open so that they cannot blink, and then household cleaners, or cosmetics, or any other products that might come into contact with a human eye are dripped into the rabbit's eye. The person conducting the test then examines the swelling, ulceration, redness, and general damage to the eye caused by the product to see if it is within certain limits. Another popular test is the LD-50 (Lethal Dose—50%) test. In the LD-50 test, many animals (usually mice or rats) are forced to ingest huge amounts of a product. The level at which half of all the animals die is the "LD-50 dose."
>
> Lest you think that these are horror stories that are unusual or rare, be assured that these are two of the most common tests done on new products. In fact, almost every new product on the market—cleaners, deodorant, shampoo, antifreeze, cough syrup, etc.—is tested in these

ways. It goes without saying that such tests cause a great deal of pain and suffering to the animals involved. I intend to argue that the pain that the animal feels must be considered in evaluating the morality of animal testing. Since animals have a right not to be caused unnecessary pain and suffering, these tests, and others like them, cannot be morally justified.

Notice that this introduction gives the context of the discussion (by explaining what animal testing is), uses some striking examples to capture the reader's interest, and presents the thesis as well as indicates why the author thinks her thesis is true. Above all, your introduction needs to be interesting enough to make the reader want to read further. Yes, your instructor is going to read through to the end no matter how boring your introduction is, but he may not read it in quite the frame of mind you desire if he's been bored senseless by your introduction. Other introductions to this topic are, of course, possible and would work equally well. As long as you include what needs to be included and leave out what needs to be left out (see the list of "don'ts" a few paragraphs back), then the form your introduction takes is a personal matter.

The Body of the Essay

When you begin to write the main body of your essay (Parts II–V in the basic outline), you need to lay out all of your premises fairly early on. If you need to provide reasons for believing those premises, do that later. First say "here is my argument," and then say "and here are my reasons for thinking that the premises are true and that the premises combine to prove the truth of the conclusion." At the outset, the reader needs to know where you are going and how you are structuring your argument and also have a general overview of the entire argument.

As you can see, the more detailed your outline is, the easier this part of the essay will be to write. In my outline for the essay on animal testing, I said, in a fairly specific way, not only what the argument was but why the premises were true. Writing that part of the essay will just be a matter of putting the pieces together with the appropriate transitions and evidence.

The body of the essay is, of course, the meat of the essay. Chapter 5 has a number of examples of different kinds of arguments, as well as ways arguments can go wrong. If you insure that you don't make any of those mistakes, you'll be in good shape. Using the sample arguments in Chapter 5 as well as other chapters and the argumentative essays that you have undoubtedly read as assignments for your course, you should have a pretty good idea of how to put together this part of the essay.

The Conclusion

There are several ways to conclude your essay. If your essay is very short (2–3 pages), you may simply end it with the final point that leads up to your conclusion. However, even short essays can benefit from a very brief summary of what you have tried to prove. Certainly if your essay is very long or complex, you should provide a summary or review of the main points of your argument. This brings closure for the reader and helps him to better follow your reasoning as well as reminding him of where you started and how you got to the conclusion.

On the other hand, your conclusion can and sometimes should go beyond just summarizing your argument. If you close with "First I said this, and then I showed how it led to that, and then I proved that between them they required that the other was true . . . ," you are going to put your reader to sleep. While you need to close with your main point, you can also go beyond it in various ways.

One way to end an essay is to show what the further implications of your thesis are. In the outline for the essay on animal testing, I indicated that in my conclusion I was going to point out that if my thesis is true, then we are going to have to change the way we live to some extent. If we can't test products on animals, then we will either have to do without some new products or we will have to put up with much slower development of medical drugs and technologies and other new products. Another possible implication, which isn't mentioned in my outline, is that there may be problems with *eating* animals, too. So another way to end the essay is to mention that what I have been arguing leads to another problem—the possibility that we should be vegetarians—but that this is a subject for another essay.

Your conclusion should certainly reflect what has been going on in the rest of the essay. You should not introduce any new information or any important new ideas at this point. If you do, you don't leave yourself room to discuss these new points, which can leave your reader hanging. But certainly you should keep your conclusion short and use your final paragraph(s) to provide a satisfying finish and a sense of completeness or closure for your reader.

CONCLUDING REMARKS

While arguing for your own theory or position is more difficult than criticizing someone else's theory, it can also be more rewarding. Of course, by creating your own argument, you open yourself up to criticism by others. Making Parts IV and V thorough and comprehensive should preempt some of that criticism. If you follow the suggestions in this chapter, your synthesis essay should be *relatively* easy to write and you should avoid any *big* mistakes.

SAMPLE ESSAY

"Why Is There a Moral Obligation to the Poor?" is an actual essay that a student wrote for one of my classes. Notice that he begins his essay with a striking quote which he then ties back to his argument in the conclusion. This is one way to begin an essay. However, take care that it doesn't end up being too "cute." In addition, his essay differs in a number of ways from the basic outline I suggested using in this chapter. In particular, he argues for a negative thesis. Instead of arguing that we do not have a moral obligation to the poor, he argues that none of the proofs claiming that we *do* have a moral obligation to the poor work. That is, he says, the arguments in favor of a moral obligation to the poor are inadequate, so it is more likely true that we *don't* have a moral obligation to the poor. Since he is arguing against other arguments, he doesn't really have Parts II and III of the basic outline. Essentially, his essay consists of Part I, extended usage of Parts IV and V, and Part VI.

I do not mean to suggest that this essay is perfect. It suffers from several flaws. The author uses emotive and sometimes inflammatory language, he sometimes ignores the principle of charity, he ignores at least one major argument in favor of obligations to the poor, and in these respects his essay should not be used as a role model. Despite these problems, this is still a good essay, in large part because the organization is so clear and provides such an excellent example of structure. One of the interesting things about this essay, of course, is that the author is arguing against an idea that most people accept. That makes his task more difficult, but he does a fine job of handling it. He is also careful not to claim to prove more than he does. Notice that he never says that we *don't* have a moral obligation to the poor, only that it isn't clear that we *do* have a moral obligation to the poor.

Here is the outline that I have extracted from his essay:

I. Introduction: I will examine three of the better answers to the question, "Why do we have a moral obligation to the poor?" and then demonstrate why each is inadequate. (Includes definition of what is meant by "moral obligation.")

II. Argument one: The "give back to society" response (society has given me both institutional benefits, like schooling and national defense, and personal benefits, like those from specific people, and thus I have an obligation to pay them back) and my objections (that is, why I think this argument is inadequate and thus fails.)
   A. Paying taxes "pays back" society for any institutional benefits I receive.
   B. Personal benefits should be paid back to the individual who gave them to us.
   C. Aren't personal benefits gifts rather than debts?

III. Argument two: The "reparation" response (because we benefit from present and past wrongs, we should repay those who suffer because of those wrongs) and my objections.
   A. Applies only to those of European descent.
   B. Do I actually benefit from child labor and slavery?
   C. This gives us no obligation to victims of natural disasters.

IV. Argument three:
   A. The "golden rule" response (if I was poor, I would want others to help me) and my objections.

B. The "luck" response (it is just blind luck that I was not born poor) and my objections.
   1. How does obligation follow from luck?
   2. Children of the rich deserve whatever benefits they receive from their parents.
V. Conclusion: None of these arguments work, so we probably don't have a moral obligation to the poor. (Includes brief mention of other possible arguments which I have ignored.)

Here's the essay:

Why Is There a Moral Obligation to the Poor?

Christopher Campbell

Now there is one word—a single word—which can blast the morality of altruism out of existence and which it cannot withstand—the word: "Why?"
                                                        —Ayn Rand, *Philosophy: Who Needs It*

INTRODUCTION

When dealing with the issue of the poor and starving of the world, moral philosophers such as Peter Singer, the author of "Rich and Poor,"[2] asks questions like: "What should be done to help the starving? How much aid am I morally obligated to give?" But in my opinion, such questions overlook a crucial issue and too easily accept a point that is very difficult to prove rationally. The issue I am talking about is summed up by asking: "Why is there a moral obligation to help the poor?"

In this paper I will examine three of the better answers to this question and then demonstrate why each is ultimately inadequate. Admittedly, there are other solutions which I have omitted. Yet the three included are those which I feel come closest to providing a sufficient answer to the question stated above. These three are:

1. The Give Back to Society Response
2. The Reparation Response
3. The Golden Rule or Luck Response

---

[2]Peter Singer, "Rich and Poor," in *Practical Ethics* (Cambridge, England: Cambridge University Press, 1979), pp. 158–91.

Before examining these in depth, however, it is first necessary to define a key term. That term is **moral obligation.** By this phrase I mean, as Singer says, "something that everyone ought to do" (262) and something that it is immoral not to do. With this established, I feel it might also be helpful to briefly explore the idea of obligation and ask: "What are moral obligations based upon?" In answer to this, I believe it is reasonable to assume that moral obligations are based upon at least two things (more are certainly possible):

1. Some good done to you that is not a freely given gift (e.g., if someone makes a loan to you, you have a moral obligation to pay him or her back).
2. Some ill or harmful act that you have done to another (e.g., if you steal and crash someone's car, you have a moral obligation to make amends for your action).

With this laid out, let us examine the three possible answers that follow and decide whether or not they are adequate to prove that there is a moral obligation to help those in poverty.

1. THE GIVE BACK TO SOCIETY RESPONSE

This response claims that our obligation to help the indigent is derived from our obligation to help society. The reason we are obligated to help society is because of the numerous benefits that we have received from it. Among these benefits are two types. The first are what I will call *Institutional Benefits,* such as military and police protection, public education, etc. The second are *Personal Benefits,* such as the kindness of fellow community members, special attention from a teacher, etc. Since the receipt of benefits leads to an obligation, we have a moral obligation to repay society. By helping the poor, we help society and thus fulfill our obligation.

Objections to Response 1

Before beginning my objections to this response, let me first say that I agree with the basis of this argument. That is, I agree that people are obligated to pay back benefits that are not freely given gifts. Thus, if it can be established (and I believe it can) that society gives its citizens things that are not intended to be gifts, then this does place upon people a certain moral obligation. I have no quarrel with this issue. What I do have a problem with is whether or not this point establishes an obligation to help the poor.

1. My first objection is that it appears that the Institutional Benefits we receive do not imply any additional obligation other than that which is met by paying taxes. In other words, by my paying taxes, I am fulfilling any obligation put upon me by accepting the benefits of public schools, paved roads, and police protection.

Yet, a traditional moralist would surely reply to this: "Your taxes do not come close to paying your actual share of the cost of such services. Thus, you still have at least a partial obligation to fulfill on the basis of these benefits."

To this I would respond in two ways. First of all, I would ask who it is who pays the portion that my taxes do not cover. The answer to this is that the rich do, by paying a great deal more than their actual share of government expenditures. Thus it follows from this that if the receipt of Institutional Benefits does imply a moral obligation to any particular group of people, it is not to the poor (as traditional morality claims) but rather to the rich.

My second response to this would be to point out that the poor pay the least of their share of the cost of Institutional Benefits, which means that the rich pick up more of their slack than they do anyone else's. Thus, the poor have the greatest moral obligation of anyone to the rich, which is quite the opposite from what traditional moralists, such as Singer, would have us believe. Thus, it appears that any response based upon giving back to society for the receipt of Institutional Benefits is insufficient (and even contradictory) to establish a moral obligation to help the poor.

2. My second objection pertains to Personal Benefits. Response 1 claims that we receive these benefits from "society," and therefore we have an obligation to repay "society." But what exactly is meant by this? While I am certainly willing to grant that human beings are social creatures and live in societies, it seems clear that our society is made up of various individuals, some who benefitted us and some who did not. If, as is clearly the case, certain individuals are the ones who have given us these Personal Benefits, why should we be obligated to some abstract concept such as society and not the individuals specifically? If I loan someone $50, she damn well better not give that amount to the Red Cross a week later and consider that my repayment. Why should our moral obligations to teachers, ministers, and others be any different?

One response the traditional moralist might give is that tracking down these individuals is very difficult, and many of them may in fact be deceased.

To this I must still ask, "How on earth does giving to a charity or a starving person on the street fulfill your obligation to a past Sunday School teacher whether you can find that teacher or not?" Unless you are giving to that teacher's favorite charity, it seems foolish to think that giving to a good cause fulfills any obligation of this kind. Thus, it appears that this response does not establish an obligation to the poor based upon Personal Benefits from society either.

3. My third objection is to ask whether or not Personal Benefits are meant to be repaid at all. Could it not be the case if, for instance, a teacher spends extra time helping a troubled student, that her efforts were meant as a gift and not a service to later be repaid? If this is the case, then any type of obligation other than gratitude cannot be expected from Personal Benefits. Thus, it appears that The Give Back to Society Response is completely inadequate for establishing a moral obligation to the poor.

2. THE REPARATION RESPONSE

This response claims that because we presently benefit from wrongs done presently, such as child labor in China, or those done in the past, like the colonialization of Africa and slavery, we have a moral obligation to repay those who presently suffer as a result of these injustices. Since these people are mostly poor, we have an obligation to help the poor.

Objections to Response 2

As with the Objections to Response 1, let me begin by stating that I agree with the principle on which Response 2 is based. If a person benefits from the suffering of others, this person has in some sense a moral obligation to those harmed. What I do question in regard to this response is whether or not it is sufficient to establish an obligation to help the indigent.

1. My first objection to this response is that it appears to apply almost solely to those of European descent. This is because if any group has benefitted from the colonialization of Africa, slavery, and the minimal wages and hard labor of poorer countries it is those of European ancestry. But to accept this implies two things. First of all, if this response is true, it appears that it is only Europeans who have a moral obligation to the impoverished. Secondly, it implies that no one has any moral obligation to a poor and starving person of European descent. While many thinkers might not have a problem with this idea, it appears that traditional moralists cannot be satisfied with such a moral doctrine because it is a far cry from establishing a universal moral obligation to aid the less fortunate, no matter who they are.

2. My second objection involves the asking of a very important question: "Just how much do I actually benefit from things like child labor in China and the past colonialization of Africa?" The answer to this question is crucial because it determines to what extent I am obligated to the Chinese children or the Africans. It would seem that most traditional moralists, when basing the idea of obligation on reparation, just assume that our moral obligation is unlimited. But is this truly the case? While it is sure that many European kings and barons got rich by taking control of Africa's many resources, it is at the very least unclear as to how much this takeover still helps me out today. The same applies to the horrendous labor conditions in China. It is certain that Phil Knight, CEO of Nike, is getting fat off the efforts of cheap Chinese labor. But how much benefit am I really getting from this? Considering the outrageous prices for tennis shoes (and other items), it appears that I am getting screwed right along with the Chinese workers. At any rate the question of how much, or even if, I really benefit from the suffering of other groups such as those mentioned above is certainly far from being answered. Thus, the question of how much, or even if, I am obligated to these groups is unanswered as well, which means that any altruistic, moral obligation cannot yet be established.

3. My third objection raises yet another important question: "Doesn't this response based on reparation still leave a great number of the poor unaccounted for?" Specifically, what of those reduced to poverty by earthquakes, famines, and floods? According to this response, there is no moral obligation to help these people. However, moralists, such as Singer, clearly believe that we are *equally* obligated to help those people as well. Thus, The Reparation Response, while it may come close, still fails to establish a moral obligation to help the poor and starving.

3. THE GOLDEN RULE OR LUCK RESPONSE

This response actually consists of two separate responses. Yet, since they are so like-minded, I include both of them here. For clarity's sake, however, I shall deal with each separately.

3a. The Golden Rule Response

This is the response that Kant uses when he says that a person cannot rationally will that there be no altruistic obligation because "many cases might occur in which one would have need of the love and sympathy [and aid] of others." In other words, you should help the poor because if you were in their situation you would want help.

Objection to Response 3a   I object to this on the same basis that I object to the Golden Rule itself. It presents obligations that, even in theory, can never be fulfilled. The wholehearted adoption of this moral rule leads to all kinds of ludicrous obligations and a total denial of the individual self. For example, if I win a million dollars in the lottery then it follows that I have an obligation to give all the money to my roommate. This is because, if my roommate won the money, I would want him to give all of it to me (whether I actually expect to get it is irrelevant, the Golden Rule stipulates that you treat others as you would *like* to be treated). Any moral idea that leads to such idiotic obligations cannot be the basis for an obligation to do anything. Thus, it is insufficient to establish any moral obligation, including one to help those in poverty.

3b. The Luck Response

This response is slightly better than 3a. It claims that my being born in a place where I have enough to eat, drink, etc. is just blind luck. I could have just as easily been born starving in a village in India. Thus, I have an obligation to help the poor, who weren't as lucky as me.

Objections to Response 3b   1. My first objection is to ask: "How does obligation follow from luck?" If I win the lottery, does my good luck mean that I have an obligation to share my winnings with all those who were not as fortunate as I? Such a moral obligation seems foolish. Thus, the link between luck and obligation appears to be tenuous at best and insufficient to establish any moral obligation to altruism.

2. My second objection is that the children of the rich are deserving of whatever benefits they received from their parents (assuming that the riches were earned and not stolen). To disagree with this is to claim that parents do not have the right to decide to give their money to their children (or anyone for that matter). Instead, The Luck Response claims that, if you are rich, people whom you have never met have a greater right to your money and possessions than do your own children. Certainly there are few who would agree with such a notion. Thus, it would seem that The Luck Response fails to establish a moral obligation to aid the poor as well.

CONCLUSION

Before ending this paper, I feel it is proper to address a likely objection. Many will claim that I have ignored a response based upon Utilitarianism or Virtue Ethics or some other moral theory. The reason that I have not included any response based upon any such moral theory is the same reason that I did not include a response based upon the poor's moral right to aid. Both of these responses, while seemingly good ones, do not actually provide a basis for moral obligation to altruism. Nearly every moral theory besides egoism is *built* upon the idea that people are obligated to help the worse off. Therefore, any appeal to them seems to me to be circular. The same is the case when appealing to the poor's moral right to receive aid. A moral right to aid for the poor is just another way of saying that there is a moral obligation to help the poor. Thus, any appeal to the right to establish the obligation is simply circular and meaningless as well.

With that explained, I feel I can more safely say that this paper, while not totally conclusive, goes a long way toward pointing out the lack of reason behind the moral theory of altruism. By asking "Why?", I feel that I have sufficiently demonstrated that the idea of a moral obligation to help the poor is not the easily acceptable given that many ethicists believe it to be.

8

USING RESEARCH IN
A PHILOSOPHY PAPER

Calvin and Hobbes

by Bill Watterson

A **research paper** is any paper for which you are expected to find and read material from sources other than your textbook. Most philosophical essays are not, and should not be, research papers. You can't go to the library to discover whether animals should be used for research, whether God exists, or whether abortion is immoral. You *can* go to the library to find out what *other* people have thought about these issues, but unless your instructor explicitly assigns a research paper, this is not what she intends for you to do. Philosophical "truths" are not things we look up in books; they are truths we acquire by a lot of hard thinking. If you merely report what someone else thinks, then you are not doing that thinking for yourself. In addition, you may be guilty of plagiarism, a serious offense that will be discussed later in this chapter.

A research paper in philosophy is generally an essay in which you take a position on some topic and then review what others have said about it. Some of them may agree with you, others will disagree. The point is, however, that a research paper is typically supposed to be original. Rarely will a professor ask you to *merely* report what others have said about your topic. Usually you are expected to present an argument for your position, and then use your research to provide counter-arguments to your position, or to present arguments in support of your position.

SOURCES

There are two different kinds of sources that you may use in your research paper: primary and secondary. A **primary source** is a book or article that is an author's own original work about your topic. **Secondary sources** are books or articles that have been written by other people *about* the philosopher or book or essay that is the primary source. In other words, if you are writing about Descartes's *Meditations,* then that book is your primary source. Your secondary sources will be books and essays in which other people write about Descartes's *Meditations.* If you look up Descartes in the *Encyclopedia of Philosophy,* you will find an article written about him. If you look up Aristotle's four causes in the encyclopedia, you will find an article explaining what the four causes are and what Aristotle says about them. These are secondary sources. If your textbook is an anthology of original sources (that is, excerpts of books or essays by Descartes or Aristotle or Mill), then those excerpts are primary sources. If, on the other hand, your textbook is the kind of book which *tells* you what Descartes or Aristotle or Mill said, then that is a secondary source.

While you will use both kinds of sources for your research paper, notice what the word "primary" means. Your *primary* source is the main or principal source for your essay. The *secondary* sources are just that—secondary. Students are often tempted to do their research in the secondary literature before they have done their own thinking about the topic. Don't do this! Even in a research paper, you should be writing an original essay and using research merely to provide support for your position. If you cram your brain with what other people have to say about your topic, there is going to be little room for you to do your own thinking. Before you begin your research, try writing a summary of what you plan to say in your essay. Once you have a pretty firm grasp on what you want to say, then you are ready to begin looking for other sources. After you begin your research, it is possible that you will change your mind about some things, but try to figure it out for yourself first.

In looking for sources, a good place to start is Appendix B, which lists a number of sources for philosophy research essays. Use the indexes in these books. Look up the author of the work you are writing about, as well as various keywords. For example, if you are writing about Descartes's *Medita-tions,* in addition to looking up René Descartes, you could also look under "Certainty," "Evil genius," "Doubt," and "Dreams," among others. *In the Ency-clopedia of Philosophy,*[1] under "Descartes, René", you will find the following:

Descartes, René 2–344, 37; 3–241

. . .

certainty 2–69

. . .

dreams 2–415

. . .

ideas 4–119

. . .

knowledge and belief 4–345, 349, 351

. . .

mind-body problem 5–336 fol., 341

. . .

skepticism 7–453

Translated, this means that you can find information about Descartes in Volume 2, pages 344 and 37, and in Volume 3, page 241. You can find infor-mation about what Descartes had to say about certainty in Volume 2, page 69; dreams in Volume 2, page 415; ideas in Volume 4, page 119; etc. Any or all of these may be helpful in writing an essay about Descartes's *Meditations.*

As another example, if you look up "Descartes, René" in the index of *The Oxford Companion to Philosophy,*[2] you will find:

DESCARTES . . . *cogito ergo sum;* doubt; . . . innate ideas; . . . *malin génie;* . . . mind-body problem; . . . scepticism, history of . . .

which tells you that you should look up each of those terms in the alpha-betical text. (The *Oxford Companion* is organized like a dictionary.)

One thing you will find, even in the books listed in Appendix B, is that you will not always be able to understand everything you read. Articles in *The Encyclopedia of Philosophy* can be rather advanced for introductory stu-dents. If you can't understand them, leave them and go look for something you can better comprehend.

---

[1]Paul Edwards, editor-in-chief, *Encyclopedia of Philosophy* (New York: MacMillan Publishing Co., Inc. & The Free Press, 1967), volume 8, p. 417.
[2]Ted Honderich, ed., *The Oxford Companion to Philosophy* (New York: Oxford University Press, 1955), p. 969.

Another thing to realize about writing research essays in philosophy is that most regular encyclopedias are relatively useless. They are often too general and sometimes too superficial to be adequate as a source. In addition, many of the sources you may have used for other classes, like *The Reader's Guide to Periodical Literature,* will be less helpful for your philosophy essay. Philosophers don't usually publish in *Time* magazine or *Redbook,* and the journals they do publish in are not indexed in the *Reader's Guide.* Even if you find something in one of the magazines indexed in the *Reader's Guide* that seems to be on your topic, chances are it is not going to be an acceptable source for your essay. *The Philosopher's Index* (see Appendix B) indexes journals of philosophy, and it can be helpful. However, there is a good chance that your university library does not carry many of the journals indexed. Also, most philosophy journals are intended for other professional philosophers and not for undergraduates. Check to see which journals your library carries. Then, as you look at *The Philosopher's Index,* you can make note of only those articles that are actually available to you.

Another place to look for sources is the library's "card catalog"—which generally is not on cards anymore. Most libraries are now cataloged on the computer, which makes searches much easier. Each book is usually listed three times in the catalog—once under the author's or authors' names, once under the title, and one or more times by subject. Search by name, topic, title, and keywords. Any computer keyword search can, of course, be tricky. You may get so many books that you don't have the time to look at them all. You can always narrow your search by adding keywords. For example, instead of searching for "certainty," you might search for "Descartes and certainty," or even "Descartes, doubt and certainty."

You need to be especially careful about the reliability of your sources. With the advent of the Internet, many students rely on the computer for all of their research. Be very careful when you read things on the Internet to be sure that the author of the information knows what he is talking about. I still remember the day one of my students called me about an essay he was writing on abortion. He started quoting "facts" about the development of the fetus, most of which were inaccurate. I asked him where he got the information, and he said, "Oh, it was on an anti-abortion web page." I gently suggested that a better source about the growth and development of a fetus might be a science textbook. It simply never occurred to him that anything he read could be wrong. While this is a very large problem with web pages, it is also a problem with some books and essays.

The moral of the story is to double-check your sources, particularly if they are making factual claims, and that applies to books, articles, and web pages. Even if the author is a famous philosopher, a professor at Harvard, or your own instructor, don't assume that she has the last word. Just because she thinks, for example, that Paley's watch analogy doesn't work, that doesn't necessarily mean that she is right. Many of the "truths" of philosophy, as I have already said, must be discovered by you. Simply because someone famous says it is true doesn't mean it is so.

QUOTATION AND PARAPHRASE

In the course of writing any philosophical essay, you will probably need to either directly quote what an author has said or paraphrase his ideas. Inexperienced writers often use quotations and paraphrases excessively. If you can state an author's point more briefly than he did, then put his main points into your own words. Quotations should be used sparingly and only for a few reasons. First, if the author has said something so eloquently that paraphrasing it would lose something from the original, then quotation is necessary. Second, if the author says something that you disagree with and want to argue against, you may need to directly quote her in order to show that you have presented her argument fairly. Third, it may be necessary to quote an author to show that he actually said what you claim he said, or to point out his use of various key words and phrases.

However, quotations can't stand on their own in an essay. If you quote a passage, you must comment on and interpret the idea. Explain what it means, why it is significant, how it fits in with the rest of your argument, and why your reader should take it seriously. The point of asking you to write a philosophical essay is to show your instructor that you understand some philosophical essay or argument. When you quote an author, all you show is that you are able to read and copy a passage. Quoting a passage does not show that you understand it.

Be very careful that your quotations aren't too long. An overlong quotation can overwhelm the point you are trying to make. Also, you want to avoid what I call a "cut-and-paste" essay, or what one teacher calls a "model plane" essay.[3] The model plane essay occurs when the writer takes a little from this source, a quote from that source, and some ideas from another source, and glues them all together with a few sentences of her own. While it can sometimes make for an elegant and clever "model plane," it's still a model plane—just like the one anyone else could put together. There is not enough in it that is original for your instructor to regard it as your own work. A paper that is merely a patchwork of other people's words will not be thought of very highly (or graded very highly) by your instructor. Here's an example of what *not* to do:

> Broad claims that judgments which profess to be about the future don't refer to any fact at the time they are made (Healey, 111), even though "it is possible for anyone who understands their meaning to see what kind of fact *will* make them true or false as the case may be" (Gale, 236). They have a present truth-or-falsity, but they are not presently true or false, "and so they *cannot* be known; there is not really anything to be known" (Dummett, 338). These statements will become true or false, Broad says, when there is a fact for them to refer to (Broad, 112).

[3]Richard Marius, *A Writer's Companion*, 3rd ed. (New York: McGraw-Hill, 1995), p. 171.

Not only does this paragraph make little sense, since it is a series of quotes and paraphrases strung together, there is no indication that the *writer* has any idea what it means either.

Think very carefully about your purpose for quoting a passage. Don't quote merely to keep from having to do your own thinking. Don't quote merely to show your instructor that you've read the book (she'll take that for granted). Above all, don't quote merely to take up space. And keep your quotations short. Any quotation that consists of two or more sentences or runs to four or more lines should be indented and single spaced, with no quotation marks. Here, for example, is a lengthy quote from Descartes's *Meditations:*

> Several years have now elapsed since I first became aware that I had accepted, even from my youth, many false opinions for true, and that consequently what I afterward based on such principles was highly doubtful; and from that time I was convinced of the necessity of under- taking once in my life to rid myself of all the opinions I had adopted, and of commencing anew the work of building from the foundation, if I desired to establish a firm and abiding superstructure in the sciences.[4]

It is usually better not to use such block quotations if you can help it. Bet- ter that you paraphrase the passage, and only use some shorter quotations if necessary.

This quotation from the passage above utilizes ellipsis marks to make the passage more concise:

> I was convinced of the necessity . . . to rid myself of all the opinions I had adopted . . . if I desired to establish a firm . . . superstructure in the sciences.

Ellipsis marks are the three little dots (. . .) used to show that something has been left out in the middle. Be careful, when you do this, not to alter the author's meaning. By leaving words out in this passage, I have not changed the meaning. However, consider the following passage, also from Descartes's *Meditations:*

> But, to this end, it will not be necessary for me to show that the whole of these are false—a point, perhaps, which I shall never reach; but as even now my reason convinces me that I ought not the less carefully to withhold belief from what is not entirely certain and indubitable, than from what is manifestly false, it will be sufficient to justify the rejection of the whole if I shall find in each some ground for doubt.[5]

---

[4]René Descartes, *Meditations on First Philosophy In Which The Existence of God And The Dis- tinction of the Soul from the Body Are Demonstrated,* from *The Method, Meditations and Phi- losophy of Descartes,* trans. John Veitch (Washington, DC: M. Walter Dunne, Publisher, 1901), "Meditation I: Of the Things on Which We May Doubt," p. 219.
[5]Descartes, *Meditations on First Philosophy,* p. 220.

Now consider the following "condensation" of that passage:

> The whole of these [opinions] are false. . . . I ought not the less carefully to withhold belief from what is . . . manifestly false.

(Notice my use of brackets to insert the word "opinions" in order to clarify what "these" applies to.) In the original passage, Descartes does not claim that all his opinions are false, nor is he merely saying that he shouldn't believe things that are false. Yet that is what the "condensed" version of the passage says. If you make any claims or assertions about Descartes's argument based on this inaccurate quotation, your conclusions are likely to be wrong because you have distorted Descartes's claims. So you can see why it is important that, when you leave words, phrases, or whole sentences out, the resulting quotation does not misrepresent the original meaning of the passage.

Never begin a sentence with a quotation mark. Quotations require lead-ins, which are your own words or phrases that tie the quotation to the rest of the text both logically and stylistically. To use the previous passage as an example, one way to use a lead-in is like this:

> However, Descartes admits that "it will not be necessary . . ."

Another example of a lead-in involves positioning a quote in the middle of a sentence, with your own words before and after it. For example:

> However, Descartes admits that "it will not be necessary for me to show that the whole of these are false," since this, he says is probably impossible.

Quotations should flow with the rest of your text and not stick out like a sore thumb. Often that means that you need to use a lead-in and/or a follow-through, by surrounding the quotation with your own words as in the example above.

PLAGIARISM

When you use someone else's words or ideas and do not properly cite them, you are committing **plagiarism.** Plagiarism is stealing, plain and simple. You have stolen the words or ideas of someone who invested his time and energy in developing them. Plagiarism is also a kind of deception: You have deceived your instructor by implying that these thoughts and ideas are your own. And finally, when you plagiarize, you wrong yourself: You have not done the work assigned and have not learned what the assignment was supposed to teach you.

Consider the two previous passages from Descartes's *Meditations*. Suppose that within the text of my essay I say the following:

> It's been many years now since I discovered that many of the things I thought were true were actually false. I realized that I needed to reject

any ideas I had that I could not be absolutely certain about. Otherwise there would be no way to be sure of anything in the sciences.

Unless this is clearly an essay about Descartes, and unless I explicitly give credit to Descartes (perhaps by beginning the passage with a statement like "Here is Descartes's main point:"), then I have committed plagiarism. By not acknowledging that this is Descartes's idea (even though I haven't used any of his exact words), I have suggested that this is my own original idea. That constitutes plagiarism.

The most common examples of plagiarism that I have come across, however, concern representing a secondary source's criticisms of an author or theory as your own. Suppose you are writing an essay about Descartes's argument in the *Meditations* concerning his own existence. Further suppose that you want to argue that Descartes is wrong and that his argument is fundamentally flawed. At this point, many students head for a secondary source to see what someone else thought was wrong with Descartes's argument. Then they write their essay using someone else's argument, without giving that person credit for the idea. This is plagiarism. You are falsely claiming that something is your own idea, when in reality you have stolen it from someone else. Even if you do not directly quote a source, you must give credit where credit is due. When you paraphrase a passage, use a citation to give credit to the author. When you borrow an idea or argument, cite the source. Otherwise, you are committing plagiarism.

Plagiarism is a serious academic offense that can be punished by failure on the essay, failure in the class, or, in the extreme, suspension or expulsion from school. Don't do it! Be sure you understand how to avoid it.

CITATIONS

Any time you use either words or ideas from something you have read, you must acknowledge the source by using some kind of **citation.** At the very least, you must mention the author's name—So-and-so claims such-and-such. If you have used the author's exact words, you must also use quotation marks. Ask your instructor which kind of citation he prefers. If he does not express a preference, follow the examples in this section.

The most common kind of citation is the **footnote.** A superscript number at the end of the quote refers the reader to the bottom of the page where the number is repeated with a citation. Here is an example.[6] Another alternative is to use endnotes. **Endnotes** look exactly like footnotes, but instead of each being at the bottom of the page, they are listed together at the end of the essay, chapter, or book.

To cite a book, whether in a footnote or endnote, you should include the author's name, the name of the essay or book, where it was published, the name of the publisher, when it was published, and the number of the page from which you quoted. Some examples follow.

[6]Notice how the footnote is at the bottom of the page to make it easy to find.

- *A single author book:*
    [1]Hugo Adam Bedau, *Making Mortal Choices: Three Exercises in Moral Casuistry* (New York: Oxford University Press, 1997), p. 56.

    According to this footnote, the material you quoted or paraphrased is found on page 56 of Hugo Bedau's book, *Making Mortal Choices.*

- *A book with several authors:*
    [2]William R. Maples, Ph.D., and Michael Browning, *Dead Men Do Tell Tales: The Strange and Fascinating Cases of a Forensic Anthropologist* (New York: Doubleday, 1994), p. 191.

- *A book with a translator:*
    [3]René Descartes, *Meditations on First Philosophy*, trans. Donald A. Cress (Indianapolis: Hackett Publishing Company, Inc., 1979), p. 13.

- *A book with an editor:*
    [4]William James, *Pragmatism*, ed. Bruce Kuklick (Indianapolis: Hackett Publishing Company, Inc., 1981), p. 36.

- *A single essay from a collection:*
    [5]Monte Cook, "Tips for Time Travel" in *Philosophers Look at Science Fiction*, ed. Nicholas D. Smith (Chicago: Nelson-Hall, 1982), pp. 54–55.

- *A journal article:*
    [6]Jonathan Harrison, "Dr Who and the Philosophers or Time-Travel for Beginners," *Proceedings of The Aristotelian Society*, supplementary volume XLV (1971), p. 24.

- *A signed article in an encyclopedia:*
    [7]A.D. Woozley, "Universals," *Encyclopedia of Philosophy*, Paul Edwards, ed. (New York: MacMillan Publishing Co., Inc. & The Free Press, 1967).

- *An Internet citation:*
    [8]Tom Buerkle, "Cloning of Humans? Unethical, EU Panel Decides." <http://www.iht.com/IHT/TB/97/tb053097.html>. May 30, 1997.

Note that for an Internet citation, the entire web address (inside the < > brackets) should be on one line. If it won't fit on one line, it should, at least, *begin* on a separate line.

When you have already cited a source once with a complete footnote reference, later citations need only the author's name and page number. Thus,

[9]James, p. 59

refers to page 59 of the James book (footnote 4). If you need to cite something not listed here, consult either Kate Turabian's excellent *Manual For Writers*[7] or *The Chicago Manual of Style.*[8]

---

[7]Kate L. Turabian, *A Manual for Writers of Term Papers, Theses, and Dissertations*, 5th ed., revised and expanded by Bonnie Birtwistle Honigsblum (Chicago: The University of Chicago Press, 1987).
[8]*The Chicago Manual of Style: for authors, editors and copywriters*, 13th ed. (Chicago: The University of Chicago Press, 1983).

An alternative to using footnotes or endnotes is to use a **parenthetical reference.** Instead of using a superscript footnote number after the quote, parentheses are used with a shortened form of the citation. If your instructor does not require footnotes or endnotes, use the parenthetical reference. It is shorter, easier to type (unless your computer word processing program does footnotes for you), and, most importantly as far as I'm concerned, it is much easier on your reader. Here is an example of a parenthetical reference using a quote from page 13 of Descartes's *Meditations:* "Several years have now passed since I first realized how many were the false opinions that in my youth I took to be true and thus how doubtful were all the things that I subsequently built upon these opinions" (Descartes 13). Notice that the parenthetical reference is placed after the quotation marks and before the period. If you use the parenthetical reference on a block quotation (which doesn't have quotation marks, remember), the reference should go after the period. If you have mentioned the author's name in your lead-in to the quotation, then the reference would just be a page number: (13). If you have two books or essays by the same author, then you should use the author's name, the year it was published, and the page number, thus: (Descartes 1979, 13). Along with your parenthetical reference, then, you will need a reference list. The form for your reference list is similar to the form of a footnote:

Descartes, René. 1979. *Meditations on First Philosophy.* Translated by Donald A. Cress. Indianapolis: Hackett Publishing Company, Inc.

The information is the same; it is just in slightly different order. The same, of course, is true for other kinds of references. So some of the earlier references would look thus:

Cook, Monte. 1982. Tips for Time Travel. In *Philosophers Look at Science Fiction,* ed. Nicholas D. Smith, pp. 47–55. Chicago: Nelson-Hall.

Woozley, A. D. 1967. Universals. *Encyclopedia of Philosophy,* ed. Paul Edwards. New York: MacMillan Publishing Co., Inc. & The Free Press.

Sources should be listed alphabetically by the author's last name.

BIBLIOGRAPHY

If you have quoted or cited any sources, you probably need a bibliography. A **bibliography** is a list of the books, articles, and journals that you have read in preparing your essay. Therefore, you may need a bibliography, even if you don't have any direct quotes. I recommend to students that *any* primary or secondary source they read to develop their own ideas and their essay should be listed in the bibliography. Even if you didn't consciously borrow any ideas, it is probably safer to go ahead and list the essay or book. If you have used the full version of footnotes or endnotes as shown above, then you may not need a bibliography. If you used parenthetical references, you will have a reference list instead of a bibliography. The form of a bibliography is slightly different from a reference list:

Cook, Monte. "Tips for Time Travel." In *Philosophers Look at Science Fiction*, ed. Nicholas D. Smith, pp. 47–55. Chicago: Nelson-Hall, 1982.

Woozley, A. D. "Universals," *Encyclopedia of Philosophy*, ed. Paul Edwards. New York: MacMillan Publishing Co., Inc. & The Free Press, 1967.

In a bibliography, as with the reference list, sources should be ordered alphabetically by the author's last name. There's not much difference between the two, and many instructors don't care either way. The key is to make sure that you give enough information about the source, so that your readers can look up the original passage if they want to. Therefore, in some form or other, you must provide author, title, editor or translator if relevant, publisher, copyright date, and page numbers. Remember, when in doubt about what form of citation or bibliography to use, check with your instructor.

CONCLUDING REMARKS

Be sure that you are careful about citing sources and including bibliographic information. Others may want to check some of your sources or even read them for themselves. By using accurate citations and references, you not only preempt any accusation of plagiarism, but you also give credit for ideas, thoughts, and theories where credit is due—that is, to their authors.

9

PUTTING PENCIL TO PAPER (OR FINGERS TO KEYBOARD)

GETTING STARTED

The most valuable piece of advice about writing essays that you will ever receive is this: Just do it. As soon as an essay is assigned, start thinking about it and planning what you want to say. Whether the paper is due next week or next month or at the end of the semester, don't wait until the night or the week before it is due to start thinking about it. Begin your research (if necessary) and your planning and organizing right away. The more you think about the essay, the easier it will be to write when the time comes. However, don't spend so much time planning and researching that you put off writing until the last minute. The sooner you begin the writing, the more time you will have for editing and revising.

Calvin and Hobbes   by Bill Watterson

CALVIN AND HOBBES © 1992 Watterson. Reprinted with permission of UNIVERSAL PRESS SYNDICATE. All rights reserved.

Make sure you completely understand the assignment. Read any instructions provided by the instructor. Ask questions. You can't write an "A" paper (or even a "B" or "C" paper) if you don't write the kind of paper your instructor has assigned. Of course, following the directions doesn't guarantee a good paper, but not following them does guarantee a poor one.

If your instructor allows you to choose your own topic, choose carefully! You need to strike a balance between a topic you find completely uninteresting and one that you feel so passionately about that you can't be objective about it. In either case, you will find it difficult to write clearly and constructively. If your instructor does not give you any guidance on possible topics, it is probably best if you choose a topic that directly relates to the material covered in class or your text. Even if your instructor does not require you to do so, you should get her approval for your topic. You don't want to spend your time writing on a topic your instructor considers unacceptable.

It is sometimes a good idea to word your topic as a question. Your essay, then, attempts to answer that question. For example, instead of choosing "Descartes's *Meditations*" as a topic (which you couldn't, in any case, cover adequately in a short essay), choose one small part of it and formulate it as a question:

> What is Descartes's ball of wax example supposed to show, and does it succeed?

In addition, it may be helpful to express your topic in a more formal way. I usually have students hand in a paper topic based on the following:

> My paper topic is _____.
>
> I intend to argue (or show) that _____,
>
> because _____.

The advantage of this format is that once you fill in the blanks, you know what your thesis or conclusion is, so you know what you need to prove in the rest of your essay. This form can be adapted to a number of the essays illustrated in this book. For example:

> Application essay: My paper topic is <u>Mill's utilitarianism</u>. I intend to show that <u>when applied to Kant's example of whether you should tell the truth to a murderer about the location of the one he wishes to murder, Mill would say that one should lie to the murderer</u>, because <u>doing so would result in the most happiness for the most people</u>.
>
> Analysis essay: My paper topic is <u>Descartes's argument to prove that he exists</u>. I intend to show that <u>he can be sure that he exists</u>, because <u>the fact that he doubts he exists shows that he must exist, since something is doing the doubting</u>.

Evaluation essay: My paper topic is <u>Paley's proof for the existence of God</u>. I intend to argue that <u>Paley's argument does not work</u>, because <u>although it provides an explanation for where the universe came from, it is ultimately unsatisfactory for a number of reasons</u>.

Synthesis essay: My paper topic is <u>whether it is morally permissible to use nonhuman animals to test products intended for human use</u>. I intend to argue that <u>it is not permissible</u>, because <u>animals feel pain and have rights, just as people do</u>.

The important thing to remember is that you can't write well about a topic that you don't understand, aren't interested in, or is either too broad or too narrow. It bears repeating—if you choose your own topic, be *sure* you check with your instructor to make sure you are on the right track.

Before you begin writing, review your class notes and any notes you took when reading the assignment. Reread the essay or argument that you are writing about. Make some notes to yourself about how you plan to proceed. If some points are not clear, consult a philosophy dictionary or an encyclopedia of philosophy (see Appendix B). Preparing an outline (see Chapters 6 and 7 for hints) is very helpful.

Finally, begin writing. Once you start, stay with it for at least an hour. Begin, keep going, and don't get discouraged. Just get your ideas on paper. However, you don't have to write the whole essay at one sitting. If it helps, begin by writing a short summary of what you intend to say—perhaps a quarter or a third the length that the essay is supposed to be. Once you get on paper the major points you want to make, you can go back and fill in the details. Don't try to edit or revise as you go along. If you can't think of the right word, just leave a blank space and keep going. If you don't like the way you've phrased something, circle it and go on. If you think a word is misspelled, circle it so that you can look it up later. Don't worry about commas, spelling, and so on, at this stage. The important thing is that you get started and continue until you have a rough draft written.

Depending on what kind of essay you are writing, consult the appropriate chapter of this book for guidelines on content. Writing a first draft isn't easy. Be sure you give yourself plenty of time. Don't worry if your first draft is wordy or rambles or doesn't seem to make the points you want to make. First drafts are expected to have problems—that's why they are *first* drafts and are followed by *second* and *third* and sometimes *fourth* and *fifth* drafts. In a first draft you are just trying to get your ideas written down. This is not the time to criticize your thoughts and arguments. Save your criticism for later revisions.

You should write your essay so that a reasonably intelligent person with no background in philosophy can make sense of it. Don't assume too much on the part of the reader. Yes, your instructor presumably knows all about the subject, almost certainly more than you do, but the point of writing an essay is for the instructor to discover what *you* know about the subject. If you assume too much knowledge on the part of your reader, your instructor can't be sure that you know what has been left out. Your job is to prove to her that you understand what she already knows. Let a roommate, spouse, sibling, or friend read your essay. If he can't understand what you are trying to say, then you need to go back and revise so that he can.

Consider writing your introduction and conclusion last. A good introduction presents your main points and indicates where your essay is going, while a good conclusion wraps it all up and shows where you have been. Realistically, you may not know exactly where your essay is going until you finish writing it. Even if you don't wait until the end to write the introduction and conclusion, you should be sure you do some serious rewriting to bring them in line with what you have actually said in the essay (as opposed to what you *meant* to say or *thought* you said).

REWRITING

Above all, don't plan to turn in your first draft. Just as you had to reread the essay or argument you are writing about, so you will have to rewrite the essay you are writing. Rewrite, rewrite, and rewrite some more. Realize, however, that rewriting doesn't mean just correcting misplaced commas or misspelled words. Rewriting means revising—that is, possibly making radical changes in your first draft. You may need to rearrange or even delete whole paragraphs. You may find that you need to add sentences or paragraphs to make your essay more intelligible. Be ruthless about removing sentences that don't fit or paragraphs that are incoherent. Don't pad your essay with irrelevancies. Don't ramble. If you did not begin with an outline, or if you have departed from your original outline, then when you finish your first draft, try outlining it. An outline will help show you where your thought processes are going wrong. Straighten out problems in organization and clarity before you begin worrying about commas and sentence fragments.

On the other hand, don't assume that grammar doesn't matter. Instructors expect correct punctuation, complete sentences, and accurate spelling. Of course, an essay that is grammatically correct and neatly typed is not necessarily a *good* essay, but don't think that having good ideas and arguments will make up for bad spelling, bad grammar, and messiness. When you do not observe the conventions of good grammar, your instructor is likely to think that you are careless, illiterate, or even dim-witted. She may also assume that you don't care enough about the class, your grade, or her to do your best work. Reading essays that are grammatically incorrect, vague, rambling, or even obscure to the point of unintelligibility is distracting, irritating, and confusing—regardless of how "profound" you think your ideas are. The fundamental goal of writing is communication with the reader and grammatical sloppiness will frustrate that goal.

After you finish a draft, put the paper aside for a couple of days, if you can. If you don't have that much time, at least leave it for a few hours. When you come back fresh to your essay, you may find that things that seemed perfectly clear originally now seem incoherent, that the connections between paragraphs are unclear or nonexistent, or even that parts of the essay are much better than you thought. Leaving the essay alone for a few days gives you a fresh perspective that can be very helpful when you begin revising.

At this point, it may be helpful to have someone else read and comment on your essay. Because you know what you are trying to say, it is sometimes difficult to get the distance necessary to be objective about your own work. Be sure that whoever reads it for you is aware of what constitutes good writing and knows the rules of grammar. Make sure the person you've asked to read your essay is willing to criticize. It won't help much if he says, "Wow, I really liked your essay." If your best friend is reluctant to criticize your writing, choose someone else. Many colleges offer free writing advice through writing centers. You need constructive criticism. Ask your reader what she thinks you are trying to say. Ask her to tell you why she agrees or disagrees with you. The point is to get some comments that will help you to improve your essay. However, don't automatically assume your reader is right. Think about her criticism carefully, but, in the end, rely on your own judgment.

PROBLEMS TO AVOID

When you revise your essay, watch out for the following common problems.

Don't Assume That Just Because Someone Famous Said It, It Must Be So

In philosophy, we are inclined to think that no one is a respectable authority. Quoting an authority is not a substitute for an argument. An authority's opinion is simply another opinion. While Kant's opinion on a subject, for example, may carry some weight, it generally isn't enough. You must provide other evidence for thinking he is right.

Use an Objective Tone

Most college papers should be written with an objective tone that avoids preachiness, inflammatory or emotional language, cliches or colloquialisms, and silliness. Many instructors will tell you never to use *you* or *I* in an essay. I instruct students not to use either one excessively, but tell them that occasionally either or both can be appropriate. Since many essays involve your opinion or evaluation of a subject, it is difficult to avoid saying *I*. However, don't get in the way of your subject. Too many *I*s indicate that the subject of your essay is you rather than some philosophical topic. If you do use *you* be sure you only use it in reference to the reader. Most uses of *you* can be revised by replacing the word *you* with *the reader* or *one* or even *they*. In any case, be sure to check with your instructor for his preferences regarding *you* and *I*. Even if he allows them, you should use them sparingly.

Use the Correct Words

Be sure that you don't equivocate on the meaning of words in your essay. If, for example, you use the words *democracy* or *communism*, be sure that you make it clear to the reader exactly what you mean by them. Chances are that the authors you quote will use these words in different ways as well. Clarify each different meaning. Unless everyone is using *democracy* in the same way, confusion will result. Benito Mussolini, for example, once claimed that his fascism was "the purest form of democracy";[1] Karl Marx said much the same thing about his socialism.[2] Obviously they are using different definitions of democracy. Unless you explain these different meanings, your essay will be incomprehensible to the reader.

Be Charitable

Remember the principle of charity discussed in Chapter 2. Give the author whose theory you are writing about the benefit of the doubt. If one interpretation of his theory seems ridiculous, and another is at least fairly reasonable, then, all other things being equal, you should assume that the latter interpretation is correct. Remember that however much you disagree with an author, he would not have written what he did if he did not think he was being reasonable. Writers often make unfair and offensive remarks or insults about a theory or idea when they don't understand it very well or they are unsure about their own position and thus feel threatened. Showing respect for an author and his work, whether you agree with it or not, is the least you can do.

Distinguish the Arguer from the Argument

Don't fall into the trap of arguing that because Jean-Paul Sartre, for example, is an atheist, then his argument for existentialism must be wrong. Don't attack the *arguer* instead of the *argument*. Sartre's atheism has nothing to do with how good his argument is. In philosophy, we are primarily interested in *arguments*. If you disagree with an author's argument, you have to work out carefully the reasons why you disagree. You can't get out of it by merely saying, "He's a lousy sort of character, so I can ignore him." This is an unfair (and unethical) way to object to an argument.

---

[1]Benito Mussolini, "The Doctrine of Fascism," in *Classic Philosophical Questions*, 8th ed., James Gould, ed. (Englewood Cliffs, NJ: Prentice Hall, 1995), p. 557.
[2]Karl Marx and Friedrich Engels, "Manifesto of the Communist Party," in *Revolution from 1789 to 1906*, R. W. Postgate, ed. (New York: Harper Torchbooks, 1962), p. 154.

Don't Use Sexist Language

Use gender-neutral language to avoid offending your reader. Instead of *mankind,* say *humanity.* Instead of *man,* say *person.* Don't use masculine pronouns when you are referring to groups that include both males and females. Instead of using *he* and *him* (unless, of course, you are talking about a specific person who is male), consider revising the sentence to use *they* and *them.* If you can't use a plural pronoun, then you should probably alternate *she* and *he.* (Notice how I have done so in this book.)

Exclude Irrelevant Facts

Students are often tempted to include in their essays historical background or personal facts about a philosopher. Unless these facts are directly relevant to the author's conclusions, omit them. On the other hand, don't exclude relevant facts just because your reader (the instructor) already knows them.

Don't Write Too Little

If your draft is too short, ask yourself: Have I clearly explained the theory or argument that I am writing about? Have I supported my main points? Have I provided arguments for why those points are correct, instead of simply stating them? Have I provided examples to illustrate my main points? If you have done all this and your essay is still too short, then your topic may be too narrow. However, if your instructor has assigned the topic, then you haven't answered some or all of these questions thoroughly enough.

Don't Write Too Much

If your draft is too long, your topic may be too broad, you may have included too much extraneous material, or you may be rambling. Longer is not necessarily better. A draft that is too long may indicate that you have very little to say about the topic and are just filling space with background or too many and too lengthy examples. Your instructor won't be fooled! On the other hand, a draft that is too long may indicate that you need to make your topic narrower. If you try to cover Aristotle's entire moral theory in five pages, you are almost certain to fail.

THE FINAL EDIT

When you have finished revising, do your final edit. The best way to edit for grammar is to read your essay aloud. Read slowly and listen to the sound of the sentences. Often your ear will detect errors that your eyes have missed. Be sure you read exactly what is on the page. Because you wrote the essay, you may automatically fill in what you meant to say. Ask a friend to read it to you while you listen, or read it into a tape recorder and then play it back. If you haven't already done so, you might want to get help from your school's writing center, if it has one.

Before you type or print your final draft, *look* at your paper. How long are your paragraphs? A good rule of thumb is that a paragraph should have a minimum of three or four sentences, but it shouldn't take up a whole page. All your paragraphs don't need to be the same length, but neither should they hit the extremes. An average page will probably have two or three paragraphs. Also, look at the length of your sentences. Shorter sentences are easier to read, but if they are too short your essay will sound like "See Spot run. Run, Spot, run." Don't make sentences too long, either. Your reader must be able to follow the sentence to the bitter end. If you have written a sentence that seems to be out of control, chances are you are probably trying to express a thought that is out of control. Divide long and complex sentences into several shorter, clearer, and more concise sentences. When you read your essay aloud, you will probably hear these trouble spots.

If you are at all concerned that a word is misspelled, look it up in a dictionary. If you are using a computer, use the spell-check function. If your word processing program includes a grammar checker as well, use it. However, don't rely too heavily on either. If you use the wrong word (but spell it right) the spell-check won't help. The spell-check can't tell if you meant *its* or *it's; their, they're,* or *there; affect* or *effect;* or *whether* or *weather.* Even the grammar check may not catch some problems. In addition, the grammar check may suggest you correct things that aren't wrong. Make use of these features, but again, don't rely on them entirely.

Be sure that your subjects and verbs agree. If one is plural, both must be. Ditto your nouns and pronouns. Don't use plural pronouns with singular nouns, or vice versa. If you are talking about one person, you must use *he* or *she,* not *they.* While we frequently use *they* to avoid sexist language, make sure the *they* refers to a plural noun.

Don't misspell the names of the philosophers or theories you refer to. The spell-check probably won't catch them, so double-check. From an instructor's point of view, it is a terrible sign of carelessness to have a student write about Descartes or utilitarianism, for example, and continually misspell the names. The first time you refer to a philosopher, use his whole name. Yes, your instructor knows to whom you are referring, but do it anyway. Also, be sure when you say, "Locke said . . . ," that it is really something Locke said and not something someone else claims Locke said.

Finally, choose a title that is descriptive of your essay. Your title should suggest the subject of your essay in a way that arouses the reader's interest. However, use common sense. If you title your essay about Descartes's *Meditations* "A Drug-induced Dream," it will catch your reader's interest, but it may not be the kind of interest you want. Titles should be relatively short, somewhat interesting, and indicative of what follows in the essay.

MECHANICS

Calvin and Hobbes   by Bill Watterson

After you have finished revising and editing your essay, you need to prepare it to be handed in. If your instructor has given you instructions, *follow them!* How you staple the pages or what kind of paper you use may seem like minor issues, but after all, the person who is grading your essay is the person who made those requests—so humor her!

If you don't own or have access to a computer, consider using the school's computer lab. Preparing a paper on a computer is much easier than typing it on a typewriter. If you use the computer lab, don't wait until the last minute to try to type your paper. Some computer labs require you to sign up in advance. Also, there are many times during the semester when the lab will be especially busy (midterms, finals, etc.). Be sure you sign up far enough in advance so that if there are scheduling problems, you can resolve them.

If your instructor has not given you specific instructions, follow these guidelines. Use 8½ × 11-inch white paper. Do not use erasable typewriter paper, other extremely thin paper, or paper in fancy colors or finishes. Make sure your typewriter or printer ribbon is printing clearly. Do not use colored ribbons. Double-space everything. Indent paragraphs five spaces.

Prepare a title page that includes your title, the course name, the instructor's name, the date, and your name. Most instructors have essays from several courses to grade. Having the course name on the title page simplifies matters for the instructor. If your instructor teaches more than one section of the same course, be sure to include the section number and the day and time your class meets, as well. Number all pages except the title page, including the bibliography, endnotes, and/or reference list, if any. It is also helpful to have your name on every page—in case one page becomes separated from the rest of the paper.

Use one-inch margins all around. Don't use huge margins in hopes that your instructor will be deceived into thinking your essay is longer than it is. Similarly, don't try to compress a long paper with small type and smaller line spacing. Don't use very large type or very small type—stick with 10- or 12-point type. Shoot for about 250–300 words per page.

Stay within the limits the instructor has set. If your essay is too short, go back and do some rewriting to bring it up to the length specified. If it is too long, cut out extraneous material. Your instructor has asked for a particular length essay because she thinks that this length is necessary to say all that needs to be said without rambling.

Unless the instructor specifies differently, staple the pages together in the upper left-hand corner. Don't use pins or paper clips or expect the instructor to supply you with staples. Use a plain, ordinary typeface. Script and other fancy typefaces can be very difficult to read. Don't use folders or fancy bindings unless the instructor specifically requests them. Your instructor will not confuse an attractive paper with a well-written one. At best, she will ignore the fancy binding or typeface—at worst, they will be a source of annoyance or distraction to her.

Proofread your essay one last time before you hand it in. Make sure the pages are in the right order and are numbered correctly. If you find errors, correct them carefully with a black pen. Be sure you keep a copy of your essay—not only on the computer, but on paper, too. If you've typed your essay, then photocopy it. Essays sometimes get lost, even by instructors.

Hand in your essay on time. If you know you will be late, speak to your instructor before the essay is due, if possible. Don't have your mother or your roommate call for you to make excuses. When your essay is returned— study it. Try to understand why you received the grade you did. Before you go to the instructor with complaints, however, wait at least 24 hours. Review what you wrote, the original work that you were writing about, and any comments or instructions from the instructor. Then, if you still have questions, make an appointment to meet with the instructor. Be sure to bring the essay with you—you can't expect her to remember all the details. Finally, good luck. If you have followed all (or most) of the advice in this and earlier chapters, then you will have made your own luck!

Appendix A
HOW TO TAKE EXAMS

There are two very important things to remember when taking an exam. First and most important is this: **STUDY for the exam.** Second, **read through the entire exam before you try to answer any questions.** A student told me once about an exam she had recently taken. There were a number of extremely difficult essay questions, which she struggled to answer in the time allotted. When she got to the last page, however, the instructor had written, "Answer only one of the preceding questions." Oops! The few minutes you spend reading over the exam are well spent for that reason, as for several others.

Other suggestions to keep in mind at exam time follow.

Read the Instructions Very Carefully

Your instructor may ask you to answer five of eight short answer questions, or two of three essay questions. You will not get extra credit for answering more (unless the instructor explicitly says so), so don't waste your time. On the other hand, be sure you answer as many as required. If you don't attempt to answer at least five of the eight, then you may lose a significant number of points.

Budget Your Time

You need to know how many points each section or question of the exam is worth. If one question is worth 50 percent of the total number of points, plan to spend half your time answering that question. If another question is only worth 10 percent of the total, you would be foolish to waste too much time on it. Figure out how much time you have to spend on each section or question, and then budget your time. If you must, stop writing when you've used up the time for that question, and move on to the next one. In general, you will get a better score if you answer all the questions at least partially than if you answer only a few completely.

Briefly Outline What You Plan to Say

For example, here is a sample question:

> We talked about several possible exceptions to the principle of autonomy. What are they? For each exception, provide an explanation of what a person who held that principle would say about legalizing prostitution.

A scratch outline might look like this:

I. Define autonomy
II. Define exceptions:
  A. Paternalism
  B. Harm principle
  C. Welfare principle
  D. Legal moralism
III. Legalized prostitution
  A. Principle of paternalism—no
  B. Harm principle—yes
  C. Welfare principle—maybe yes or no
  D. Legal moralism principle—no

By making a quick outline, you insure not only that your essay is somewhat organized, but also that you answer everything asked. I have used this question on several exams, and almost inevitably, several people answer everything except the part about legalized prostitution. That is a big part of the answer I expect, because applying the principles to the issue of prostitution shows me how well the student actually understands those principles.

Think Before You Write

Read all the questions and answer the one you know most about first (but be sure to keep your eye on the clock, so you don't spend too much time on it). While you are answering the questions you are most sure of, your subconscious may be working on the others. Also, answering one question may spark something relevant about one of the others.

Answer the Question That Is Asked

If your instructor asks you to define a term, define that term. Don't define some other term or pad your answer with related but irrelevant information. Answer the question asked, and make sure you answer the entire question. Essay questions often have several parts, and if you answer only the first part, you will automatically lose points. So be sure you read the entire question carefully.

Use Your Outline to Write Your Answer

Because you are under a time constraint, you will not be able to write the kind of essay you could write out of class. Among other things, that means you should probably forget about any introduction or conclusion. Jump right in with the answer. For example, for the earlier question on exceptions to the principle of autonomy, your essay should probably begin something like this: "According to the principle of autonomy . . ." You can't write a perfect essay in 15 minutes or even in 50 minutes. Your instructor does not expect it. He does expect you to answer every required question, and every part of each question. He also expects that your exam will be readable—so don't write so carelessly that he can't decipher it. In addition, you need to pay attention to grammar, because although he will not expect it to be letter-perfect, he will expect it to be coherent.

Don't Worry About Revising or Editing

You may not have time to revise or edit. Try not to stop in mid-sentence, but do move on to the next question when the time you have allotted is up, so that each question is at least partially answered. Most instructors give partial credit on essay exams, so writing something is almost always better than writing nothing. If you really don't know the answer—guess. It is better to try rather than not. Go back and revise after you have answered all the questions, if you have time. It is a good idea, when you are deciding on how many minutes to devote to each question, to give yourself a little leeway of five minutes or more. Those few minutes should give you time to proofread your answers. When you are under time pressure, it is easy to leave out words, to write down one name when you mean another, and to misspell words and names. It is better to spend a little less time on each question, in order to use the time saved to proofread.

Don't Pad Your Answers, but Do Include Relevant Examples

Even if the instructor doesn't ask for an example, giving a brief one can help to show that you understand the concepts. Try not to use the same examples your book uses or that your instructor has used in class. Again, if the question on autonomy had not referred to legalized prostitution but had asked only for definitions, including a brief example when you define each principle could help show you know what you are talking about. Here is a relevant piece of the answer to that question:

> The principle of paternalism says that we can violate a person's autonomy in order to prevent him from doing something that will harm himself. For example, a person who accepts paternalism would be in favor of preventing people from committing suicide. The harm principle says that we can stop people from doing things, if what they are doing is going to harm someone else. So a person in favor of the harm principle would be in favor of preventing rapes, murders, and assaults.

Notice that the examples are very short, but long enough to demonstrate that you know how to apply the principle.

Use Your Own Words to Express the Ideas

Sometimes, you have heard a particular principle so many times that you can quote it verbatim. For example, once learned, most students can quote the principle of utility: "An action is right in proportion as it tends to promote happiness and wrong as it tends to produce unhappiness." That isn't a direct quote (quite), but it is very, very close to the original. If you are asked what the principle of utility is, and that is all you say, your instructor has no way of knowing if you *understand* what it means. Put it into your own words, and provide examples. You may have to use more words than the original principle and it may not sound as elegant, but it will provide your instructor with a much better idea of whether you understand what you are writing.

Bring and Use the Kind of Pencil or Pen Your Instructor Requests

If he does not tell you beforehand, bring both pencil and pen. Use only blue or black ink—fancy colors are distracting and can be hard to read. Plus, if you write in pink or red, then the instructor's notes and corrections may not show up very well. Plan to bring paper to the exam, even if the instructor doesn't tell you that you will need it. If the instructor requires that you use a blue book, bring at least one and preferably two or three, in case you need more space or some other problem develops.

Be as Neat as You Can Be

Since you are writing under a time constraint, your instructor won't expect perfection. However, she will expect that your exam will be easily readable. If you use paper to write your essay questions, instead of a blue book, make sure you staple the pages together in the right order. After answering a question, leave the rest of the page blank so that if you need to add something to it later, you'll have room. If you must mark out a sentence or paragraph that you don't want in your answer, mark it clearly and completely by drawing a single line through it; don't scribble all over it and make a mess trying to hide what it says. If you are allowed to use pencil, do! That way you can erase mistakes instead of marking them out.

Show Up for Class on the Day Your Instructor Returns and Discusses the Exam

Look over the exam carefully to discover what you did right and what you did wrong. Don't simply look at the grade and then throw it away. Keep the exam at least until you get your final grade for the class. If you have any questions about your exam or about any comments the instructor made on it, make an appointment to see him to go over it. But before you do that, go back and compare your exam to the text to see if you can figure out for yourself what you did wrong and why.

Finally, Don't Panic

An exam is simply an exam, and in most classes a bad grade on one exam will not cause you to flunk the class. A poor performance on an exam does not mean you are a terrible person, that you are going to fail the course, or that you will never achieve true happiness. Keep it in perspective. It is just an exam.

Appendix B
USEFUL PHILOSOPHICAL SOURCES

Philosophy Dictionaries

This should be the first resource you consult when you begin to look for references. There are many dictionaries of philosophy available. Which ones your library has is anyone's guess. However, one good one (which isn't actually called a dictionary and is more like a short encyclopedia) is *The Oxford Companion to Philosophy.*[1] Anthony Flew's *A Dictionary of Philosophy,*[2] Simon Blackburn's *The Oxford Dictionary of Philosophy,*[3] and Robert Audi's *The Cambridge Dictionary of Philosophy*[4] are also good ones. There are also specialized dictionaries for various subfields of philosophy.

Encyclopedias of Philosophy

The Encyclopedia of Philosophy[5] is an eight-volume work that your library is likely to have. However, there are many others available. Again, go to the library and look. Check the card catalog under Philosophy—Encyclopedias and Dictionaries. Be aware that some of these encyclopedias will be too difficult for introductory students. If you don't understand what you are reading, try another encyclopedia. Or go to a good philosophy dictionary and read the reference in it, to see if it helps you understand the encyclopedia reference better. There are also specialized encyclopedias—for example, of ethics, bio-ethics, religion and philosophy, and so on. Browse the reference section to see what else is available.

[1]Ted Honderich, ed., *The Oxford Companion to Philosophy* (Oxford: Oxford University Press, 1995).
[2]Antony Flew, *A Dictionary of Philosophy,* rev. 2nd ed. (New York: St. Martin's Press, 1979).
[3]Simon Blackburn, *The Oxford Dictionary of Philosophy* (Oxford: Oxford University Press, 1996).
[4]Robert Audi, ed., *The Cambridge Dictionary of Philosophy* (Cambridge: Cambridge University Press, 1995).
[5]Paul Edwards, ed., *The Encyclopedia of Philosophy* (New York: Macmillan, 1967).

Several good reference works are available on the Internet, including the Internet *Encyclopedia of Philosophy*, which can be found at: <http://www.utm.edu/research/iep>, and the *Stanford Encyclopedia of Philosophy*, which can be found at <http://plato.stanford.edu>. Or check out one of the following web sites:

Religion and Philosophy Resources on the Internet
<http://web.bu.edu/STH/Library/contents.html>

Philosophia: Portmore's Annotated Guide to Philosophy on the Internet
<http://humanitas.ucsb.edu/~portmore/links.htm>

Philosophy in Cyberspace
<http://www.geocities.com/Athens/Acropolis/4393/>

The History of Philosophy

There are many single and multivolume works on the history of philosophy. Some of the ones that are most likely to be in your library are the following:

Frederick Copleston, S. J., *A History of Philosophy*, Volumes 1–9 (New York: Image Book, 1985).

W. T. Jones, *A History of Western Philosophy*, 2nd ed., Volumes 1–5 (Fort Worth: Harcourt Brace Jovanovich, Inc., 1980).

Bertrand Russell, *A History of Western Philosophy: And its connection with political and social circumstances from the earliest times to the present day* (New York: Simon & Schuster, 1960).

Journals of Philosophy

Journals are published regarding practically every topic or subfield in philosophy. Again, what is available to you in your college library will vary. Most of these journals are indexed in *The Philosopher's Index*,[6] which is available in quarterly volumes or on CD-ROM. In addition, the *Index* catalogs books, book reviews, anthologies, and individual articles from anthologies. Each book or article is indexed by both subject and author. Before you go to the *Index*, however, check to see what journals your library carries. Many libraries carry only a limited selection of philosophy journals, so don't waste your time discovering great references in the *Index*, only to find that you don't have access to the right journals.

Philosophy journals are filled with articles written by professional philosophers *for* professional philosophers. That is, very few of them are geared toward undergraduate students, and many of the articles may be too difficult to understand. Find which journals your library carries and go check out a couple of issues. If they are too difficult, ignore them. Some articles in some journals may not be too difficult, so you might want to at least try. Don't give up without at least checking.

---

[6]Richard H. Lineback, ed., *The Philosopher's Index* (Bowling Green, OH: Philosophy Documentation Center, 1967).

Introductory Texts

One good source to start with may be an introductory philosophy text. In fact, if your library resources are limited in the way of dictionaries, encyclopedias, or historical texts, you may have to rely on introductory texts. Many of them are anthologies of primary sources, which often have explanatory introductions to the readings. An even greater number of introductory texts are secondary sources that explain to you what the philosopher meant, how his arguments work, and what his theories are. However, see Chapter 8 on the subject of evaluating sources. All introductory texts are not created equal, so don't accept that any one particular text is correct. If you find the same material in several places, then you can be more confident that the source is accurate.

Here are some good introductory texts:

S. E. Frost, Jr., *Basic Teachings of the Great Philosophers,* rev. ed. (Garden City, New York: Doubleday, 1962).

Ben-Ami Scharfstein, *The Philosophers: Their Lives and the Nature of Their Thought* (New York: Oxford University Press, 1980).

Samuel Enoch Stumpf, *Socrates to Sartre: A History of Philosophy* (New York: McGraw-Hill, Inc., 1993).

Max Hocutt, *First Philosophy: An Introduction to Philosophical Issues* (Belmont, CA: Wadsworth Publishing Company, 1980).

Nigel Warburton, *Philosophy: The Basics,* 2d ed. (London: Routledge, 1995).

Several more lighthearted and amusing, cartoon-based general introductions to philosophy include:

Donald Palmer, *Does the Center Hold? An Introduction to Western Philosophy,* 2nd ed. (Mountain View, CA: Mayfield Publishing Company, 1996).

Donald Palmer, *Looking at Philosophy: The Unbearable Heaviness of Philosophy Made Lighter* (Mountain View, CA: Mayfield Publishing Company, 1988).

Richard Osborne, *Philosophy for Beginners* (New York: Writers and Readers Publishing, Incorporated, 1991).

Logic Texts

If you need more help on deductive and inductive arguments, informal and formal fallacies, emotive language, and the like, try one of these books:

Patrick J. Hurley, *A Concise Introduction to Logic,* 6th ed. (Belmont, CA: Wadsworth Publishing Company, 1997).

S. Morris Engel, *With Good Reason: An Introduction to Informal Fallacies,* 4th ed. (New York: St. Martin's Press, 1990).

Howard Kahane, *Logic and Contemporary Rhetoric: The Use of Reason in Everyday Life,* 6th ed. (Belmont, CA: Wadsworth Publishing Company, 1992).

Appendix C

GLOSSARY

amnesia   Loss of memory, often due to brain injury.

analogy   An "argument by analogy" claims that since two things are similar in some ways, they are similar in some other important, significant way.

analysis   Reducing a complex whole (like an argument) into its simpler, component parts.

appeal to authority   Claiming that a statement is true on the basis of what some authority says.

appeal to unqualified authority   A fallacy that occurs when the "authority" cited is not an authority on that subject.

application   To apply a theory, *argument,* or principle to a new situation or scenario.

argument   A group of statements (called *premises*), one or more of which claim to provide proof, support, and/or reasons to believe another statement (called the *conclusion*).

argumentative essay   One in which some argument is presented—either an original argument in favor of some conclusion, or an argument explaining why some argument is wrong (*see Chapters 6 and 7*).

Aristotle   (384–322 B.C.) Greek philosopher, student of *Plato*. Extremely influential especially over the medieval philosophers. Known for, among other things, his *virtue theory* of ethics, and his *four causes.*

Aristotle's four causes   Aristotle claimed that when we ask why something is the way it is, we are actually asking four different questions. We want to know what the "cause" of the thing is, but "cause" for Aristotle is closer in meaning to our "because." Why is the marble sphere the way it is? (1) Because the sculptor made it (the *efficient* cause—what brought it into existence); (2) because it is a sphere (the *formal* cause—its shape or form, whatever is essential to its nature); (3) because it is marble (the *material* cause—what it is made of); and (4) because it is to be admired (the *final* cause—its purpose or aim).

assumption   Something we take to be true, without any *argument* or *justification*.

autonomy   The idea that people should be allowed to make their own choices, to choose the kind of person they want to be and the kind of life they want to lead, to be self-determining, without interference from others. We violate a person's autonomy when we prevent him from doing what he wants to do and/or force him to do something that he does not want to do.

ball of wax example   *Descartes* used this example to show that there must be some physical substance that is not dependent on shape, smell, taste, or other characteristic. Imagine, he says, a ball of wax. It is relatively round. It has recently come from the bee hive and it still smells sweetly of clover. If you reach out your tongue, a bit of honey is still adhering to it and it tastes sweet. It is firm and cold and if you tap on it with a knuckle it makes a thumping sound. Now suppose you move the wax closer and closer to the fire. What happens? It begins to get warm and loses its shape. The heat burns up the fragrance and sweet taste. Eventually what you end up with is a pool of liquid wax. Yet it is the same object it was before we melted it. Thus, Descartes says, there must be something that is "wax" that is not dependent on shape, smell, taste, etc.

bibliography   A list of all the books or articles consulted or referred to in an essay or article.

capital punishment   The practice of executing prisoners who have committed crimes that are considered to be appropriately punishable by death.

casuistry   A method for the resolution of questions of right and wrong by applying general moral principles to particular cases.

causation   The relationship between an act and its effect; the process by which an effect is produced. If two events are causally related, then when the first (*the cause*) is present, the second (*the effect*) must also occur.

certainty   Occurs when some belief is beyond rational *doubt;* that is, when a belief cannot be doubted.

citation   A *footnote, endnote,* or *parenthetical reference* giving credit to the person whose words or ideas are used.

cogent inductive argument   An *inductive argument* that is *strong* and has true premises.

cogito ergo sum   Latin for "I think, therefore I exist." This is *Descartes's* famous conclusion at the end of the second meditation in *Meditations on First Philosophy,* which is the starting point in his search for *certainty.* Whatever else he might be mistaken about, he thought, the one thing he could be sure of was that as long as he was thinking, he must exist. Even if he is doubting all his beliefs— even if he is mistaken about all his beliefs—something must be doing the doubting, something is mistaken, and that something, that *I,* must exist.

communism   The theory that advocates a classless society, where each person works according to his abilities and receives goods and services according to his needs. Also opposes ownership of private property.

conclusion   What the *premises* in an *argument* are supposed to be providing proof or support for.

consequentialist   In *ethics,* a consequentialist is one who thinks that what makes an action right or wrong depends on how good or bad its consequences are. If an action has good consequences (results) then it is morally right. If an action has bad consequences, then it is morally wrong. Contrast with *deontological* theories. For a *deontologist,* telling a lie is always wrong. For a consequential- ist, telling a lie will only be wrong if it results in bad consequences. If good con- sequences result, then telling a lie will be the right thing to do.

counter-argument An opposing *argument* to show why some other argument is wrong.

counter-example An example used to show that some *argument,* principle, or the- ory is wrong by substituting terms that make the *premises* true and the *conclu- sion* false.

deductive argument An *argument* in which the *premises* are claimed to support the *conclusion* in such a way that if all the premises are true, then the conclu- sion must also be true.

democracy The form of government in which the people themselves, or their elected representatives, hold the political power to create laws, run the govern- ment, etc.

deontological From a root word that means "obligation" or "duty." An ethical the- ory that claims that the results or consequences of actions are irrelevant. All that is relevant in determining what is morally right is to determine what your duty is.

deontologist One who holds a *deontological* ethical theory.

Descartes, René (1596–1650) French philosopher and mathematician. Famous for his method of *doubt,* which led him to the *cogito ergo sum.*

design argument The argument for the existence of God which claims that because the universe shows evidence of design, it must have had a designer. One famous version of this is *William Paley's* watch argument. Suppose you were walking on a deserted beach and you came upon a watch. Would you suppose that the watch just happened? That the laws of metallic nature just came together in a certain way, and the watch was created? Or would you assume that *somebody* designed the watch? Clearly the watch wasn't just an accident; its complexity shows that some intelligent being designed and created it. How much more complex than the watch is the universe? If the watch had a designer, doesn't it follow that the universe must have had one as well?

dilemma Strictly speaking, a dilemma involves a situation where you have only two incompatible choices, and both seem to be obligatory. In addition, both may be equally unattractive for some reason. For example, when telling the truth would cause harm to someone but telling a lie also seems to be wrong, you are caught "between the horns" of the dilemma. For example, see the *homicidal maniac* case.

doubt To doubt something may mean either to believe that it is false or to be uncertain about the truth of it.

dreams One of *Descartes's* reasons for doubting what he thinks he knows.

egoism The theory that says either that people always do act in their own self- interest (psychological egoism) or that people ought only to do what is in their own self-interest (ethical egoism). The ethical egoist says that the morally right thing for me to do is whatever will be best for me.

emotive language Language that expresses feelings or emotions and intends to induce those feelings in the reader or listener.

empiricism   The view that everything we know (besides mathematics and logic) we must learn through experience, through our senses. For example, if we cannot see or hear or touch God, then, according to the empiricist, we cannot know that God exists. Contrast with *rationalism*.

empiricist   A person who believes in *empiricism*.

endnote   A *citation* found at the end of a chapter or book.

epistemology   Theory of knowledge. One of the main branches of *philosophy* that asks and attempts to answer questions like: "What do I know?" "What can be known?" "What is the difference between knowledge and belief?"

equivocate   Using a word or phrase to mean two different things.

ethics   One of the main branches of *philosophy* which studies right and wrong, good and bad.

euthanasia   Literally, "a good death." The practice of allowing patients who are dying and/or in a great deal of pain that cannot be relieved to refuse treatment and die, or even to help those patients die by giving them a fatal injection, for instance.

evaluation   Providing your opinion of how good or bad an argument is, along with reasons for why you think so.

evil genius   In French, *malin génie*. One of *Descartes's* three reasons for doubting everything he thinks he knows. Suppose there is a genius, as powerful as God but evil, so that he is always deceiving me about what I see or hear, or whether 1 + 1 = 2, or anything else I think I'm sure of.

example   An instance that illustrates a principle, argument, or theory. In the previous definition (of the *evil genius*), "1 + 1 = 2" was an example of the kinds of things *Descartes* thought the *evil genius* might be deceiving him about.

existentialism   School of philosophy that emphasizes both freedom and responsibility. Existentialists claim that we are totally free (as in never being caused to act by heredity, environment, or personality) and thus we alone are responsible for our actions.

expediency   Suitable for achieving a particular desired result. When *John Stuart Mill* talks about actions being "expedient," he means that they will result in happiness.

extension   The extension of a thing is its dimensions in space. A thing has *extension* if it takes up space. Bodies have extension, ideas don't.

fact   A fact is usually seen in opposition to a belief or an *opinion*. A fact is something that can be proved, for which supporting documentation can be produced. A belief or opinion cannot be proved in the same way. When a fetus's brain begins to develop is a fact; whether or not it is right to abort a fetus is an opinion.

fallacy   A fallacy is a mistake made in an *argument*. Usually it is one that *seems* correct but isn't, often because of ambiguities in grammar, the meanings of words, or the inclination to be convinced by reasons that are not good ones.

false cause fallacy   A fallacy that occurs when the conclusion of an argument depends on a causal connection that probably doesn't exist.

false dichotomy or **false dilemma fallacy**   A fallacy that occurs when only two alternatives are presented, but in fact some third alternative is possible.

feminism, feminist A group of philosophical theories (usually political and/or ethical) that (1) are largely based on the premise that at least some parts of our society are exploitive of and unjust to women and (2) advocate change.

footnote A *citation* found at the bottom of the page on which the words or ideas are cited.

formal fallacy A mistake in reasoning that occurs because there is something wrong with the form or structure of the argument.

four causes See *Aristotle's four causes.*

gender-specific Usually, the use of masculine pronouns when talking about groups of people that include both men and women.

greatest happiness principle *John Stuart Mill's* ethical theory (*utilitarianism*) which states that the right action is the one that leads to the greatest amount of happiness for the greatest number of people.

harm principle The principle that we may violate a person's *autonomy* in order to prevent him from harming other people.

homicidal maniac *Immanuel Kant's* famous example: Suppose a friend tells you that a murderer (the homicidal maniac) is chasing him and wants to kill him. Your friend asks if he can hide in your basement, and you agree. Pretty soon, the homicidal maniac comes knocking at your door, waving a gun around and asking you where your friend is. Do you tell the homicidal maniac the truth or not? Kant says that your duty is always to tell the truth. If your friend ends up dead because you told the truth, it's not your fault. You did your duty, which is the only important thing. See also *deontological.*

Hume, David (1711–1776) Scottish philosopher and historian. As an *empiricist,* Hume believed that the only things we can know are what we learn through our experience or our sense perceptions, and that our "self," for example, is just a bundle or collection of those sensory perceptions.

imperfect duties An imperfect duty, according to *Immanuel Kant,* is something that I must do (hence it is my duty), but there is not some identifiable person or group who has a right to expect me to do it. Contrast with *perfect duties.*

indubitable, undoubtable An indubitable idea is one that it is impossible to doubt.

inductive argument An argument in which the *premises* are claimed to support the *conclusion* in such a way that if the premises are true, the conclusion is probably true as well.

informal fallacy A mistake in reasoning that is not a matter of the form or structure of the argument, but can only be identified by examining the content of the argument.

innate ideas Ideas that we are born with, that don't come from experience or education.

invalid deductive argument A deductive argument in which it is possible for all the premises to be true and the conclusion to be false (having to do with the form of the argument).

is/ought fallacy A mistake in reasoning that occurs when the arguer moves from saying that something *is* the case to saying that it *ought* to be the case.

James, William (1842–1910) American philosopher and psychologist, known for his theory of *pragmatism.*

Judeo-Christian God   The God of the Jewish/Christian Bible. See *"3-O"* God.

justice   Fairness and impartiality of treatment; also, the idea that people should get what they deserve.

justify, justification   To justify a statement means to provide reasons and arguments to show that it is true.

Kant, Immanuel   (1724–1804) German philosopher. Known for his *deontological* ethical theory.

killing   Killing something or someone usually implies that some action has been performed that caused the death.

legal moralism   The idea that the purpose of the law is to enforce morality. Thus we can violate a person's *autonomy* any time we think that what they are about to do is immoral.

letting die   Letting someone die (as opposed to *killing* them) usually implies that something has *not* been done, which, if it had been done, would have prevented the person from dying. Thus, I let someone die when I don't give her medicine that could save her life.

Locke, John   (1632–1704) English *empiricist.* Known for, among other things, his theory of *personal identity,* which claims that what makes us who we are is our memory of having been that person.

logic   A branch of *philosophy* that is concerned with correct reasoning and the evaluation of *arguments.*

lying   Intentionally saying something that is not true in order to deceive.

malin génie   See *evil genius.*

Marx, Karl   (1818–1883) German philosopher and social theorist. Known for his theory of *communism.*

Meditations   René *Descartes's* work entitled: *Meditations on First Philosophy In Which The Existence of God And The Distinction of the Soul from the Body Are Demonstrated.*

metaphysics   A branch of *philosophy* primarily concerned with what kinds of things exist and what their nature is (e.g., God, time, minds, etc.).

Mill, John Stuart   (1806–1873) English philosopher. Known primarily for his doctrine of *utilitarianism.*

mind-body problem   Concerns what connection there is between the mind and the body. Is the mind simply the result of firing neurons in the brain, or is it something completely distinct?

moral theory   See *ethics.*

morally equivalent   Two actions are morally equivalent if they are equally deserving of praise or blame. If two actions are morally equivalent, then it cannot be the case that one of them is good and the other is bad.

Mussolini, Benito   (1883–1945) Italian fascist premier.

necessary   A "necessary truth" is a statement that must be true—that cannot be false. A "necessary condition" is one that has to be true in order for something else to be true. For example, being an animal is a necessary condition for being a dog, because nothing is a dog, unless it is also an animal.

necessary conclusion In a *deductive argument,* a *conclusion* is necessary when the *argument* is *valid* and all the *premises* are true.

opinion A belief that is not supported by evidence. Contrast with *fact.*

Paley, William (1743–1805) English theologian and philosopher. Famous for his version of the *design argument* that proves the existence of God.

parenthetical reference Used instead of *footnotes* or *endnotes* to cite a source. For example: (Descartes 13). Used after the quotation marks but before the period.

paraphrase To put the ideas from a sentence or passage into your own words.

paternalism The principle that we may violate a person's *autonomy* in order to prevent him from harming himself.

perception Anything we receive through our senses (sights, sounds, etc.).

perfect duties A perfect duty (according to *Kant*) is a duty that I have, that some other person has a corresponding right to expect me to perform. So, for example, I have a perfect duty not to lie to people, since each and every individual person has a right not to be lied to by me.

personal identity Whatever it is that makes me who I am. Is it my mind, my body, my memories, my perceptions, or what?

philosophy Comes from Greek words meaning "love of wisdom." In general, it is a field of study (like biology or mathematics) in which what is studied are the most basic principles—Does God exist? What is time? Who am I? What is good? Includes such subfields as *ethics, epistemology, metaphysics,* etc.

plagiarism Using someone else's words or ideas in such a way as to imply that they are your own.

Plato (428?–?348 B.C.) Ancient Greek philosopher, student of *Socrates.* His writings are some of the first attempts to answer the questions of *philosophy.*

political philosophy The branch of *philosophy* that is concerned with what the right kind of government is and various other political issues.

pragmatism A school of *philosophy* (associated with *William James,* among others) which emphasizes the practical application of ideas and truths. A belief, James says, is true if it is useful and benefits the believer.

premise The reasons, evidence, and/or justifications given to show that a *conclusion* is true.

primary sources A primary source is an author's own writing about a topic. A *secondary source* is one that explains what an author said about the topic. So a primary source is *by* the author, and the secondary source is *about* the author and/or his arguments.

principle of charity When we read an author's words, we should interpret them in such a way that makes them most likely to be true and plausible.

principle of utility See *utilitarianism.*

probable conclusion When a conclusion is probable, it means that you can't be absolutely certain that it is true—it is only probably true. See *inductive argument.*

proof A proof or demonstration of a statement is a *sound/cogent argument* with that statement as the conclusion. See also *argument.*

quotation When you use an author's exact words. Note that they should be surrounded by quotation marks (" ").

rationalism   A philosophical movement usually contrasted with *empiricism*. A rationalist believes that knowledge comes from the use of our reason, and not through our senses and experience.

reference list   A list of all the books, articles, essays, etc. that have been cited in *parenthetical references* in the body of an essay.

research paper   Any paper for which you are expected to find and read material from sources other than your textbook.

rhetoric   Persuasive, flamboyant, or elaborate language. Usually used in contrast to genuine *argument*, implying that it is *mere* persuasion, without reasons and evidence to back it up.

Sartre, Jean-Paul   (1905–1980) French philosopher. Known primarily for his theory of *existentialism*.

secondary sources   See *primary sources*.

sexist   To show attitudes involving discrimination and oppression on the basis of sex.

skepticism   The view that knowledge is not possible. If I am skeptical about the occurrence of miracles, then either I don't believe that miracles occur, or else I don't think we can ever be justified in believing that miracles occur.

socialism   A theory that advocates a classless society and public ownership of the means of production, but which is distinguished from *communism* by the fact that benefits and burdens of society are unequally distributed according to the individual's contribution to society.

Socrates   (470?–399 B.C.) Greek philosopher whose ideas were recorded by *Plato*. Extremely influential because of his "Socratic dialogue"—a method of discovering the truth by a series of questions and answers.

sound   A sound *deductive argument* is one in which the argument form is *valid* and all the *premises* are true.

straw man fallacy   A fallacy in which an argument is caricatured or misrepresented in order to make it easy to refute.

strong inductive argument   An *argument* in which the *premises* provide only probable support for the *conclusion*. Thus the conclusion is not guaranteed to be true; it is only more likely to be true than it is to be false.

summary   An attempt to put the main ideas and arguments of an essay or passage into one's own words. Distinguished from *paraphrase* by the fact that a summary is usually considerably shorter than the original and is concerned with only the most important points of the essay.

superscript   A small letter or number that is placed above the level of the other words. For example:[3].

syntax   The way words are put together to form phrases and sentences; having to do with the grammar or form of a sentence.

synthesis   A synthesis essay brings together parts and elements of several theories to create a new whole that requires original thinking.

tabula rasa   Latin for "blank slate." *John Locke* argued that when we are born, our minds are "blank slates," which means that we are not born with any innate ideas.

term   Usually a noun or a noun phrase, which can be used as the subject of a sentence.

thesis A thesis statement is usually the conclusion of an argument—that is, it is the idea that an essay argues for or tries to establish.

3-O God A God who is *O*mnipotent (all powerful), *O*mniscient (all knowing), and *O*mni-benevolent (all good).

uncogent inductive argument An inductive argument in which either one or more of the premises are false or the argument form is *weak,* or both.

understanding essay An essay meant to show not only that you know a particular concept or theory, but also that you understand what it means.

universals Abstract things like truth and beauty and love (as opposed to physical things like people and tables). The problem of universals is whether these are mere concepts or ideas that exist only in our minds, or whether they are actual things that exist in the world.

unsound deductive argument A deductive argument in which either one or more of the premises are false or the argument form is *invalid,* or both.

utilitarianism The ethical theory that states that an action's rightness or wrongness depends upon whether the consequences of the action lead to happiness or unhappiness. A morally right action is one that produces happiness, and a morally wrong action is one that produces unhappiness.

utility For a philosopher, it means more than just usefulness; it means the amount of happiness something produces. See *utilitarianism.*

valid deductive argument An argument that has a structure or form such that whenever the premises are true, the conclusion must also be true.

virtue theory An ethical theory that is more interested in the question, "How can I be a good person?" than in the question, "What is the right thing to do?"

weak inductive argument An inductive argument whose premises do not provide good reasons for thinking the conclusion is even probably true.

welfare principle The principle that we may violate a person's *autonomy* in order to force him to help other people.